THE REGENT

The REGENT

Dale Perelman

THE FITHIAN PRESS · SANTA BARBARA · 1990

To Michele for all her support.

AuthorHouse™
1663 Liberty Drive
Bloomington, IN 47403
www.authorhouse.com
Phone: 1-800-839-8640

Published by AuthorHouse   05/30/2012

ISBN: 978-1-4772-1341-4 (sc)
ISBN: 978-1-4772-1342-1 (e)

The REGENT

TABLE OF CONTENS

Vast images of ages past
shine through its pure white light.
What secrets would the Regent cast,
if only stones could write.

A PARISIAN SUMMER drizzle hurried my steps through the doorway of the Louvre offices. Inside the building, an elevator carried me upstairs to meet with Daniel Alcouffe, the Louvre Museum's Curator of Arts and Antiquity. Earlier in the day, Monsieur Alcouffe and I had discussed the Regent Diamond for more than an hour. Now, I returned with my wife to photograph the stone.

Monsieur Alcouffe's secretary motioned us to the curator's office. As our host greeted us, a bell signaled the Louvre's closing for the day.

"A moment please," Monsieur Alcouffe spoke in heavily accented English. He picked up the telephone and murmured in French. Within the minute, a uniformed guard entered the room.

"If you are ready, we can go," Alcouffe paused momentarily. "Please, no flashes."

"Yes," I answered, thankful for his help. "We understand."

The three of us followed the guard through the dimly lit corridor of the office complex to the museum proper. I marveled at the exquisite paintings lining the walls. As the guard stopped to unlatch a large carved wooden door, James McNeill Whistler's

"Arrangement in Grey and Black Number 1" greeted us from the opposite wall.

"Look Michele, Whistler's Mother," I told my wife. She nodded her head in recognition.

"Monsieur, you may enter the *Galerie d'Apollon*," the curator said.

Although I had visited this room on numerous occasions to view the Regent Diamond, entering through the hidden side doors across from Whistler's masterpiece added a new dimension. Charles LeBrun had designed the gallery in 1661 under the reign of Louis XIV. The ornate murals, carved wooden doors, somber wall paintings and parquet floors rivaled any European palace in the world. The nineteenth century ceiling painting of Apollo vanquishing the serpent by Eugene Delacroix and the murals of the four seasons seized my immediate attention.

After absorbing the rococo splendor of the room, my eyes moved to the decorative floor cases. A beam of light from the clouded sky sneaked through a window guiding me to Vitrine VII, which contained the 20-carat pink Hortensia diamond, the 55-carat Sancy, the *Cote-de-Bretagne* ruby, and the 140¾-carat Regent Diamond. As the spotlight above the glass case highlighted the perfect whiteness of the Regent, centuries of history cascaded through my mind. I imagined Louis XV, Marie Antoinette, Napoleon Bonaparte, Charles X, and Empress Eugenie wearing this diamond, and I knew I had to write the story of the Regent.

ONE

GREAT EVENTS had begun to shape Mother India during the opening of the eighteenth century. The English East India Company had gained a foothold in the south at Madras while Hindus and Moslems struggled for control to the north. However, these countervailing historical forces played little effect on the daily lives of the downtrodden Hindu workers who populated the country.[1]

Until his hand first brushed against the diamond, the Sudra never considered the inequalities of human life. Rather, as a member of the lowest caste and as a practicing Hindu, he accepted the reality of day to day pain as part of his existence. He believed if this world were difficult, the life to come would surely be better. He refused to blaspheme the gods and lived simply and uprightly according to his religion. How this diamond would change his life![2]

Working in the mines under the sweltering heat of the Indian sun caused the Sudra's toothless mouth to grow dry. His forehead oozed thick globules of sweat. As the tiny Hindu's calloused fingers discovered the sharply-defined surface of a huge diamond buried a few inches beneath the mud, he became mesmerized by the thought of the riches this stone could bring. His black eyes sparkled with the intuitive delight of a man who knew the critical moment in his life had arrived.

Years of hard work in the mines had aged the Sudra prematurely, but his dreams carried him through each day's

hardships. Whenever his bruised body ached and trouble over-
whelmed him, his mind would carry him back through the
years to his boyhood when an old soothsayer in his village,
called the "All-Seeing One," had predicted some marvelous
event would shape his life. Surely, she referred to the mammoth
diamond beneath his fingers.

"You have the mark of fortune upon your brow," the withered
old hag had prophesied. "When your moment comes, grasp it
firmly. Dig your nails deeply and hold on with all your strength.
Do not allow Mother Fortune to escape."

The Sudra remembered the soothsayer's words. His moment
had come. He would steal the diamond from the mine.

The year was 1701. The Sudra had toiled his entire adult life
in Emperor Aurangzeb's diamond quarries. Aurangzeb, "Grasper
of the Universe," the last of the great Mogul rulers, was a strict
Moslem fanatic with little love for his "infidel" Hindu subjects.
His intolerance insured a difficult life for the Hindu workers.[3]

More than sixty-thousand men, women and children labored
in the emperor's diamond mines one hundred and fifty miles
south of the region known as Golconda, today called Hyderabad.
The Sudra worked along the bank of the Kistna River in the
Parteal Mine.

Mines were divided into small individual claims operated
by local Hindu laborers who paid a percentage of any gem-
stones unearthed to their Moslem overlords. Overseers carefully screened each miner's take to insure the largest and finest
stones found their way to Emperor Aurangzeb's treasury at
Delhi.[4]

Each miner cleared an area adjacent to his claim and surrounded it with a wall of mud. After loosening the gravel in
his claim, he poured the diggings into the separate walled-in
area for drying and sorting. The miner carefully raked these
diggings to expose the larger clumps of rock that were broken
up with a wooden pestle. Following this process, he winnowed
the exposed material with straw baskets. The lighter gravel
would be blown away, and the heavier gem-bearing ore sunk to
the bottom. During a final step, the worker picked any precious

stones from the baskets by hand and presented them to the Moslem overseers for tabulation.

Had the Sudra found the diamond in the walled-in area, the Moslem overseer who stood by his claim most certainly would have seen him. Luckily, the Sudra first discovered the stone in the center of his claim. Years of experience made his fingertips instantly recognize the diamond's octagonal outline. Since the diamond was nearly the size of his fist, the Sudra knew it must be a monster stone, the largest he had seen. Chills of excitement ran up and down his back.

This illiterate and superstitious Sudra, barely five feet tall with pock-marked face and uncomplicated mind, viewed the world in elementary terms. The legends from his village convinced him diamonds dropped from the sky during rain storms, transformed and crystalized by the violent electrical action of thunderbolts. If the skies were black and overcast, any resulting diamonds would be flawed or misshapen. If the skies were clear, the diamonds would be as white as pure river water.[5] Somehow, the Sudra knew this stone would be perfect.

From the moment he first touched the diamond, the Sudra yearned to possess it. Why should this wonderful gift belong to Emperor Aurangzeb, a cruel and violent despot who had initiated the dreaded "jazia" or religious tax on all Hindus? Surely, the gods would condone the theft as just retribution against such a tyrant. The rest of the day the Sudra, shuffling dirt while pretending to go about his work in the mine, plotted the theft of the great stone.

The following morning, the Sudra steeled his resolve. The diamond would be his. He selected a spare turban and wrapped it around his left thigh. Then, feigning a serious injury to his upper leg, he limped to his claim past a Moslem overseer. Since one Sudra looked much like another to the guard, he failed to notice the Hindu's changed condition.

During the early part of the day, the Sudra worked his way to that special spot to check his prize. He reached beneath the mud. Yes, the diamond was still there. Moving a few feet to his left, the miner routinely worked. As noon approached, the Sudra paid little heed to the blazing Indian sun that burned his back and shoulders. The diamond preoccupied his mind.

Shortly before dusk, the Hindu moved to the spot where the diamond lay. Reaching into the gravel, he stealthily eased the diamond between his legs into the bandage. Although the stone bit into his skin, the Sudra stoically suffered. Tiny droplets of blood seeping through his makeshift bandage added the proper degree of realism.

"All right you heathens," snorted the overseer. "Home, the lot of you."

The miners began to stow away their tools for the night. The Sudra wiped his brow with a nearby cloth. He placed the pestle and winnowing basket in a container. He worked slowly to avoid any unusual attention. An agonizing death would be his penalty if caught.

Luckily for the Sudra, the theft went well. He took the stone and proceeded along the bank of the Kistna River toward the coastal city of Masulipatnam, where he hoped to sell the stone to an English sea captain reputed to do anything for money. If all went well, he would share the proceeds from the stone with the Englishman in exchange for the stranger's help.

The bandit-infested pathway along the river bank terrified the Sudra. Fear of discovery by Emperor Aurangzeb's troops presented a constant danger. Sweltering heat burning the back of his neck, mosquitoes biting his face, and sharp stones tearing his feet made the journey oppressive. After several days of such torture, the Sudra welcomed the coast. Following yet another day of seeking information from the inhabitants of Masulipatnam, he found himself inside a small inn. There, the English captain he sought stood at the bar gulping a mug of punch concocted from sugar, lime juice, spice, water and arrack, the local spirit.

"Sahib," pleaded the Sudra, subserviently approaching the Englishman. "Grant me a moment."

The burly sea captain with the fierce eyes and coal-black beard glared at the inconsequential intruder who dared interrupt his revels. "What do you want, scum of the earth?"

"Sahib, I can make you a rich man."

"You, make me a rich man? Dare you jest with me, you filthy dog?"

"Sir, it is true I am dirty. I have traveled many days across this hot and dusty land to see you. Please, let us speak in private."

"Very well," conceded the captain, somewhat amused by the Hindu. However, the captain's amusement quickly changed to earnest interest when he viewed the diamond.

"Blimey mate, where did you get that bloody stone? Stole it from the old Mogul's mines if I don't miss me guess. It must be worth a fortune; aye, even a kingdom. You little varmint, you're a thief."

The Sudra nodded in silence.

"Well, what do you want of me?"

"Captain Sahib, take me to Madras aboard your ship. You can sell this diamond to one of the gem merchants. They will not question a white man. Then, we can share the profits. Both of us will be rich."

Following a few quick words, the captain and the Sudra reached an agreement. However, the arrangement troubled the unscrupulous captain's innate sense of greed. He possessed the ship to take both of them to Madras. He had the connections required to sell the diamond. Why should he share the profits with this Sudra?

The next morning, shortly after daybreak, the captain, Sudra and crew boarded ship. The waters of the Bay of Bengal appeared unusually rough. Monsoon season would soon begin.

"Looks like we be in for some weather, sir," shouted the mate to the captain.

"The weather will hold til Madras. I'm sure of it. Luck is with us today," answered the captain, who all the while was fingering the large diamond buried in his coat pocket. "Cast off."

A few miles out to sea, the captain ordered two members of his crew to bind the Sudra and toss him overboard. The tiny Hindu struggled against his captors, but the burly sailors were too strong.

"Why do you do this, Captain Sahib? We had an agreement," cried the Sudra with the shrill tremble of betrayal etched in his voice.

"Life is cheap. Throw him in the drink," the captain ordered. Within the minute the Sudra found himself in the water.

As a shark circled around him, the unfortunate Hindu cried out against his fate. Was this the great event the soothsayer had prophesied or merely Emperor Aurangzeb's revenge? How bitterly the gods had dealt with him.

Suddenly the Sudra's body stiffened, and he felt a sharp tear in his thigh at the very spot where the diamond previously had cut into his skin. The shark had struck.

"Aye," screamed the Sudra, looking toward the rapidly disappearing ship. "A curse upon you and all your children. May the goddess Kali poison your final days with a bitter death."

As the captain watched the Sudra sink beneath the deep blue waters, he slowly exhaled a puff of smoke from his pipe and watched it rise toward the sky. With only the slightest pang of regret, he looked back toward the water. The Sudra was gone.

At Madras, the captain sold the diamond for 1,000 pounds, or approximately $5,000, to a gem dealer named Jamchund. The captain immediately began to spend his newly found wealth on riotous living. Always a heavy drinker, he began to indulge more than ever.[6]

Soon, terrible thoughts began to trouble the captain. At night, visions of Kali, the Hindu goddess of death and destruction, a hideous four-armed, blood-stained creature who dressed in a girdle of snakes, a necklace of skulls, and earrings of corpses, began to haunt his dreams. In one hand, she held a human head; in another, a bloody knife. With her two other hands she beckoned the captain to come closer. Her eyes glowed with the madness of hashish while her tongue slithered between her sharp fangs like a poisonous cobra. All the while, the Sudra sat by Kali's side and silently glared at the captain.

Each night grew worse. The more terrifying the dreams, the more the captain drank. Soon the days became as restless as the nights. Relentless thoughts of Kali haunted every waking moment. The captain's fear grew into madness, and the drinking offered little solace. One night, the captain hanged himself. His contorted body was found with a horrible grimace carved across his bloated face. The Sudra had been avenged.

As to the diamond, the gem dealer Jamchund realized he had made an excellent purchase from the English sea captain. The four-hundred-and-ten-carat uncut diamond possessed the finest color and had but one slight flaw. Jamchund called the diamond the "Milliona," because of its value. Only a very wealthy man could afford to buy this stone from him. Jamchund resolved to sell the prize to Thomas Pitt, the English governor of Fort St. George at Madras for a tidy profit.

TWO

"HE WAS A SCOUNDREL and a rogue," observed one of Thomas Pitt's contemporaries, "but a damned fine specimen of a man." His life consisted of a string of adventures. Pitt was born on July 5, 1653, in Blandford in the county of Dorset, England, the second of nine children of a country parson. Following his father's premature death in 1672, the nineteen-year-old Pitt left the serenity of his home to seek his fortune in foreign lands. He enlisted in the merchant marine as a mate aboard the *Lancaster*, an East-Indian vessel under the command of Captain Goodlad.

A violent disagreement with his captain caused the always volatile Pitt to desert ship at the city of Balasore on the Bay of Bengal. Shortly thereafter, Pitt met Richard Edwards, the manager of the English East India Company's factory at Balasore, in a local pub.

"You say Goodlad is a rough one," said Edwards, gulping down a mug.

"Aye, that he is," answered Pitt. "Worked me night and day without a decent rest for hardly a farthing. I plan to be a man of account, and I'll be little more than a slave if I remain his mate."

Recognizing Pitt's potential usefulness, Edwards introduced the youth into the service of his cousin, Matthias Vincent, chief of affairs for the Company at Hugli. Pitt's career blossomed under his new employer, a man with few scruples whose ambition rivaled that of Pitt. In 1679, Pitt married Jane Innes, a niece to both Vincent and Edwards, whose dowry gave him what he called "the good working tools" to advance his own wealth. While supposedly purchasing sugar in Persia for the Company's stores, Pitt traded goods on his own behalf, multiplying Jane's dowry into a large personal fortune. Pitt and Vincent continued to pursue every potential opportunity to parlay their earnings regardless of Company interests. When Rumors of such conduct leaked back to England, the Company fired Pitt and Vincent.[7]

Both men had implicated themselves in numerous scandals throughout the years. In 1673, a man named Hall accused Vincent of murdering Rugo Podar, a Hindu commodity broker. Although the courts acquitted Vincent, many in the Company questioned his innocence. The authorities had associated Thomas Pitt with desertion, interloping and piracy since his arrival at Balasore.

In addition to dismissing Pitt and Vincent, the Company demanded a thorough investigation of their activities. The officers ordered their agent, Sir William Hedges, "to seize upon the person of Mr. Matthias Vincent, our late chief in the Bay, and send him forthwith a prisoner." Furthermore, Hedges had been ordered to confiscate Vincent's books and records as evidence of the "abuses, frauds, and injuries that have been done by him." The Company warned Hedges to be especially wary of Pitt, "he being a desperate fellow and one that we fear will not stick at doing any mischief that lies in his person." Company officers in England directed their attorney to file suit for punitive damages against the two.

Fearful of the Company's justice, Pitt and Vincent escaped Hedges to find refuge with the Dutch trade mission in India. The Dutch allowed the two men to trade freely, adding to their fortunes. Faced with more pressing problems elsewhere, the Company decided to drop criminal charges against Pitt toward the end of the year. Recognizing he could return home with impunity, Pitt arrived in England a wealthy man. Although the courts levied a 1,000-pound fine against Pitt for his previous interloping, the Company took no further action.

Throughout the next decade, Pitt lived quietly in England as a country squire and respected citizen. He was already the father of one son, and his wife gave birth to two more sons and two more daughters. In 1687, recognizing Pitt's upgraded position and the possibility for future service, the Company forgave his past actions, rebating 600 of the 1,000-pound fine. The following year, the Company directors elected him to membership without the customary fees. Shortly thereafter, Thomas purchased the manor at Stratford near his birthplace and was elected to Parliament. Thomas Pitt's life in England had been fruitful.

In contrast, the Company had been less fortunate. Charges of bribery against several officers resulted in the House of Commons calling for an immediate end to the East Indian monopoly charter. Effective leadership became crucial to the Company's continued existence in India. The directors demanded prompt action.

During the next Company shareholder meeting, one of the officers nominated Thomas Pitt as a candidate for Governor of Fort St. George. Several directors became outraged at such a suggestion, remembering his days as an interloper. Past-Governor Child called him "a roughling immoral man," and rough he was. A short, thick-set, broad-shouldered man, he resembled an English bulldog. His granite chin, wide nose with open nostrils and weathered face testified to great physical strength. Pitt swaggered rather than walked. His fits of temper created constant tension with those around him. Although his character suffered many ailments, few questioned his ability to command. Thomas Pitt was charismatic.

On November 24th, 1697, following a heated discussion, the directors elected Thomas Pitt as Governor of Fort St. George to succeed Nathaniel Higginson. Pitt was in his mid-forties and comfortably rich. Most men would have contented themselves with his accomplishments, but Thomas Pitt was an extraordinary individual. He possessed ambition enough to forsake the security of England for the brutal climate of India in pursuit of greater power and wealth.

On January 5th, 1698, Pitt became President of the Company's affairs on the coast "of Coromandel and Orissa, and of the Gingee and Mahratta countries and Governor of Fort St. George and Fort St. David" at a nominal salary of 300 pounds per year. He arrived in India on July 7th with his oldest son, Robert.

Pitt's responsibilities at Fort St. George proved onerous. With only a handful of soldiers, he protected several hundred English civilians and a native population in the thousands. The fort itself measured only four hundred by one hundred yards. The outside walls provided limited protection from direct assault. Four bastions and corresponding batteries represented the fort's only defenses. Survival in that unfriendly land required all Pitt's stubborn determination.

Fort St. George's geographic location made life especially oppressive. The city was bounded by rough seas on one side and a muddy river on the other. During the winter months, the sea assaulted the ships in the bay, while in the monsoon season, the river threatened to swallow the city. When summer came, the ground surrounding the fort became dry and infertile. Fruits and vegetables refused to grow, and the ravages of disease and fever posed a constant danger.

However, the proximity of Fort St. George to Golconda's diamond mines in the north created a strong inducement for Pitt and other council members to speculate in gems. Pitt previously had learned about diamonds from the book *Travels in India*, written by the famous French traveler, Jean Baptiste Tavernier, the foremost authority on Indian stones. During his more than eighty years, Tavernier purchased diamonds in India from the Mogul rulers and sold them to Louis XIV and other European dignitaries. The Frenchman's technical descriptions of diamond cutting and proportioning whetted Pitt's taste for more knowledge. The sketches of Emperor Aurangzeb's fabulous diamonds transported the Governor to a world of fantasy. Pitt dreamed of owning one of the giant diamonds mentioned in Tavernier's journal. How wonderful it would be for a poor parson's son to possess the 280-carat Great Mogul or the fabulous blue diamond Tavernier sold to Louis XIV!

The Company permitted its officers to trade in diamonds to augment their low salaries. However, gem speculation involved a high degree of risk. The diamond market demanded both shrewd bargaining skills and thorough information on pricing. Native cutters artfully concealed flaws from unknowing buyers. In a letter to Sir Stephen Evans, the court jeweler to Queen Anne, Pitt described a technique whereby "the Brahminies greas'd a stone to hide the fowles." In addition to fraud, the potential for theft, piracy, and shipwreck increased insecurity. In fact, Pitt once lost a magnificent fifty-eight-and-one-half-carat stone when a ship sank at sea. Even if a diamond reached the safety of England, its owner gambled on the talent of his cutter and the conditions of the economy. Many a fine piece of rough had been shattered into hundreds of pieces by inadequately trained cutters. Likewise, wars and depressions had decimated diamond investments.

On October 18th, 1701, Pitt wrote Sir Stephen Evans, alluding to an exceptional diamond that was "dear in price." A few weeks later, the gem dealer Jamchund showed that very stone to Pitt. When the Governor expressed a mild interest, the Hindu gem merchant presented him with a glass model for closer examination. By the time he left the Governor, the gem dealer felt certain he would sell the stone.

"I have him now," announced the well-dressed Hindu to his everpresent companion and friend, Vincatee Chittee. "The Governor is a dogged man, and I have whetted his appetite. He hungers for my diamond and will not rest until he gets it. I shall feed it to him at my price." Jamchund paused to smile, and the tiny lines around his mouth crinkled. The gem dealer pointed toward his friend's mouth, and the two men laughed at Jamchund's joke. "You see, my friend, I shall offer the stone for 200,000 pagodas. If I am correct, the Governor will pay 50,000. That will sooth his hunger and line my pockets." Jamchund placed his hand on Vincatee's shoulder, and the two men burst into laughter.

On November 6th, 1701, Pitt again wrote his friend Sir Stephen Evans:

> This [letter] accompanies the model of a stone I have lately seen; it weighs Mangelins 303, and carats 426. It is of an excellent crystaline water without any fouls, only at

one end in the flat part there are one or two little flaws
which will come out in cutting, they lying on the surface
of the stone. The price they ask for it is prodigious,
being two hundred thousand pagodas; tho I believe less
than one would buy it. If it was designed for a single
stone, I believe it would not lose about 1/4 part in cutting,
and be a larger stone than any the Mogul has, I take it.
Pro rata as stones go I think 'tis inestimable. Since I saw
it, I have been perusing of Tavernier, where there is no
stone so large as this will be when cut.[8]

Upon receipt of Pitt's letter, Evans cautioned his friend:

We are now in a war. The French King has his hands
and heart full, so he can't buy such a stone. There is no
Prince in Europe can buy it, so would advise you not to
meddle in it.[9]

However, the distance from England to India slowed Evans
reply by several months. In truth, Pitt's desire for the stone
overcame him. Yielding to temptation, he purchased the stone
without waiting for Evans' answer. In correspondence to his son
Robert, Pitt described the purchase in complete detail:

I heard there were large diamonds in the country to be
sold which I encouraged to be brought down, promising
to be their chapman if they would be reasonable therein;
upon which Jamchund, one of the most eminent diamond dealers in those parts, came down and brought
with him a large rough stone, about 305 mangelins, and
some small ones, which myself and others bought. But
he asking a very extravagant price for the great one, I
did not think of meddling with it, when he left it with
me for some days, and then came and took it away
again: and did so several times, insisting upon not less
than two hundred thousand pagodas, as I best remember.
I did not bid him above thirty thousand, and had little

thoughts of buying it, for that I considered there were
many and great risks to be run, not only in cutting it,
but also whether it would prove foul or clean or the
water good; besides I thought it too great an amount to
be ventured home on one bottom. But Jamchund resolving to return speedily to his own country, so that I best
remember, it was in February following, he came again
to me (with Vincatee Chittee, who was always with him
when I discoursed him about it) and pressed me to know
whether I resolved to buy it, when he came down to
100,000 pagodas, and something under, before we parted,
when we agreed upon a day to meet and make a final
end thereof one way or other, which I believe was the
latter end of the aforesaid month, or the beginning of
March. We accordingly met in the consultation room,
where after a great deal of talk, I brought him down to
55,000 pagodas, and advanced to 45,000, resolving to
give no more, and he likewise resolved not to abate, so
delivered him up the stone, and we took a friendly leave
of one another. Mr. Benyon was then writing in my
closet, with whom I discoursed what had passed, and
told him now I was clear of it, when about an hour after,
my servant brought me word that Jamchund and Vincatee
Chittee were at the door; who being called in, they used
a great many expressions in praise of the stone, and told
me he had rather I should buy it than anybody: and to
give an instance thereof offered it for 50,000. So believing it must be a pennyworth if it proved good, I offered
to part the 5,000 pagodoes that was then between us,
which he would not hearken to, and was going out of the
room again, when he turned back and told me I should
have it for 49,000. But I still adhered to what I had
before offered him, when presently he came to 48,000,
and made a solemn vow that he would not part with it a
pagoda under; when I went again into the closet with
Mr. Benyon, and told him what had passed, saying that
if it was worth 47,500 it was worth 48,000, so closed with

him for that sum, when he delivered me the stone, for which I paid him very honourably."

Thus, Governor Thomas Pitt purchased the stone his family came to call the "Pitt Diamond" for 48,000 pagodas, a sum approximating 20,400 English pounds or $100,000.00. With the acquisition, Pitt's problems magnified. Popular legend associated large diamonds with bad luck. Pitt's later years would testify to such a curse. The Governor's early exhilaration of ownership quickly crumbled beneath anxieties for the stone's safety, coupled with insinuations he had unfairly obtained the diamond.

Until his death, Pitt's enemies accused him of stealing the gem from a Jamchund. Even the sharp-tongued poet Alexander Pope pointed his barbed finger at Pitt in *Man of Ross:*

Asleep and naked as an Indian lay,
An honest factor stole a gem away;
He pledg'd it to the knight, the Knight had wit.
So kept the diamond, and the rogue was bit.

Adding to Pitt's woes, the despotic and sometimes irrational Mogul Emperor Aurangzeb declared an immediate end to further English trade in India. One of Aurangzeb's generals, Daud Khan, set siege to the nearby city of St. Thome. Danger threatened Fort St. George as well. The Governor recognized he had to get the diamond out of India at once. He selected his twenty-two-year-old son, Robert, for this important mission. Pitt recognized many shortcomings in Robert. The Governor viewed his son's extravagance with grave misgivings. In one letter to Robert, Pitt wrote: "All your actions seem to be the product of a hot head and giddy brain."

In return, Robert felt little fondness for his father. He abhorred his father's bluntness and lack of education. The Governor's violent temper terrified him. Robert also disliked India. He missed the excitement of polite society and planned to return to England aboard the *Bedford.* The elder Pitt chose Robert rather than trust the stone to a stranger. However, doubting the seaworthiness of the *Bedford,* the Governor urged Robert to book

passage on the *Loyal Cooke* instead. The Governor's judgment
would prove justified when the *Bedford* sank and the crew
drowned several months later.

On October 9th, 1702, Robert departed Fort St. George carrying
his father's letter of instructions:

> Having made Sir Stephen Evans and you my attorneys,
> revoking all others, I earnestly desire you to be careful
> of my business.
>
> I must also desire you to write me by all conveyances
> whatever advising what relates to public and private
> affairs. And whereas I have entrusted under your care
> what is of great value, which you must by all means and
> diligence preserve, let what accident will befall you,
> which God deliver you from; and if you should have the
> misfortune, which God forbid, to be taken by an enemy,
> you must be sure to throw overboard every paper you
> have, and secure *it* in the best manner you can and be
> careful afterwards that you are not discovered.
>
> But if it pleases God that you arrive safe in England,
> I strictly charge you not to stir out of the ship til Sir
> Stephen Evans or Mr. Alvarez comes on board, and
> would have you write from the first port you can send a
> letter to Sir Stephen Evans, desiring him to meet the
> ship as soon as possible, till when you will remain on
> board. You must also be very careful of this concern on
> board the ship at sea and in harbor.

If legend can be believed, Robert hid the diamond in a
special compartment in the heel of his boot. As the Pitt Diamond
sailed closer to England, the Governor's fears multiplied. Appre-
hensive about the stone's safety, Pitt bombarded his son with
correspondence. On October 15th, less than one week after his
son's departure, Pitt wrote:

> I received no letter from you after you got aboard. I
> hope you will not be so forgetful of my instructions and

the good advice I have often given you. I hope this will
meet you arrived safe at St. Helena, or in England, with
what I have committed to your charge, which I hope
will be well disposed of by you and those I have joined
with you. The true value I must never expect; but I
hope you will never part with it for much less. I gave
you an account how to estimate the value, which I hope
you are master of.

It is no small charge that I have entrusted you with,
being the management of all my affairs. Be sure not to
let slip any opportunity of writing. My credit as well as
interest depends very much on the prudent management of yourself. If any be inquisitive (I mean Sir Stephen
or Mr. Alvarez) what that cost, you may tell them about
130,000 pagodas. If the thing be kept secret and well
managed, it must yield an immense sum of money.

The diamond had possessed Pitt's soul, becoming both his
blessing and curse. The steamy Indian nights grew long and
sleepless. Strange dreams troubled him in his bed as he imagined
every possible nightmare. An undulating sea serpent with fiery
red eyes wrapped its body about the *Loyal Cooke* and dragged
the ship beneath the ocean depths. Pitt watched with horror as
his son gasped for air, and the diamond disappeared forever.
Awakening with a start, Pitt shuddered. Sweat poured through
his nightshirt, soaking his bed.

Daytime gave the Governor little peace. His life became
constant pressure. Internal bickering between members of his
staff combined with native belligerence began to wear heavily on
the Governor.

Thoughts about the diamond occupied what little free time
Pitt possessed. He contemplated the potential size and value
of the finished stone. The French gem expert Tavernier's
journal indicated a one carat flawless fine white diamond
should sell for eleven pounds and five shillings at that time.
Diamond values supposedly increased geometrically with size.
Therefore, Pitt anticipated his rough diamond would yield

a finished gem of at least 280 carats, a stone as large as the Great Mogul Diamond mentioned in Tavernier's journal. Using the Frenchman's formula, Pitt estimated the final value of the cut diamond at 879,245 pounds, or somewhere around $4,000,000.00.

The Governor realized his venture involved a high degree of risk. The Pitt Diamond might make him one of the world's wealthiest men. However, if the diamond were damaged or stolen, the result would be catastrophic.

In January, The Governor wrote Alvares Da Foncesca, a diamond merchant whom he called Mr. Alvarez in his letters:

> The consignment I made to Sir Stephen Evans, Your Self and My Son I hope came safe into your hands, and that 'twill answer in goodness to the full as I represented it. The King of France or Spain will in all probability be the likeliest chapmen for it, unless our Parliament, upon good success in some noble undertaking, will be so generous as to buy it for the Crown of England. I have left it to your discretion whether you'll make a single or two stones of it, but remember don't part with it without its full value, which must be very considerable.

The following day, Pitt penned a second letter to Evans, Alvarez, and his son:

> I have lately for my diversion been perusing Tavernier, whose method of calculating the value of great stones I observe; and if what I sent you, being made a single stone and when cut will weigh about 300 carats, according to his calculation, it would be worth 800,000 pounds. How that calculation will hold in the present time I am to seek, and therefore depend upon your knowledge and integrity.
>
> I doubt not you will take care that it be lodged in a secure place and if the times will not admit of your selling it at its full value, I hope you will be very cautious of letting it go out of your own possession.

You may be sure I think daily of this matter, and upon
often meditating thereon, I am of opinion that it be kept
entire, and if you think fit to cut it, I believe it will come
out a clean stone of about three hundred carats, which I
hope may be worth at least fifteen hundred pounds per
carat.

With each day, the Governor's distress intensified. Months
had passed, and he had yet to receive a letter from Robert. "Fie
upon him," mouthed Pitt. "That boy wants proper responsibility
to his father. How dare he ignore my commands?" The Governor's
face reddened. His stomach burned from the churning acids.
When Pitt's anger eventually softened, he imagined the possibility of some catastrophe. What if his son had drowned at sea?
Could French pirates have seized the *Loyal Cooke?*

The diamond and his son's safety preoccupied his thoughts.
Pitt had difficulty concentrating upon his work. When rumors
of the *Bedford's* loss at sea reached Pitt at Fort St. George, he
became despondent. Had the *Loyal Cooke* indeed suffered the
same fate?

Surely, something terrible had happened to Robert. His son
had set sail from India in October of the previous year. The
month of May approached, and Pitt had yet to hear from his
son. Being a pragmatic man, he prepared for the worst.

"By God, he's dead! I know it. My son is dead," Pitt moaned.
The hint of a tear formed beside the Governor's eye. "The
diamond's lost, and I am ruined."

THREE

SUMMER PASSED, and the Governor awaited news from his son. Pitt's life in India had become hellish. The Mogul Emperor Aurangzeb, vowing to destroy every foreigner in the land, created an atmosphere of fear among the English at the fort. The Governor's short temper aggravated his subordinates, who sabotaged his authority at every opportunity. His irritability alienated him in a sea of turmoil, where worries about his son and the diamond's safety caused him even greater anguish.

While the Governor stewed in India, his flighty son Robert arrived safely in England. Shortly after reaching London, the youth fell in love with a young woman named Harriet Villiers, the sister to the Earl of Grandison. Preoccupied by Harriet, Robert ignored his father's "great concern."

On May 27th, after several months in England, Robert wrote his father about his engagement while failing to mention the diamond. As he read Robert's letter, Governor Pitt's stomach ached and his forehead bristled. Pitt's hearty appetite had caused his once firm body to deteriorate and grow flabby. The Governor inhaled with difficulty while fuming at his son's thoughtlessness. His chest pounded. His heart thumped with anger. Furiously, he penned a reply to Robert demanding a thorough explanation concerning the diamond.

On December 30th, 1703, after more than a year, the lovesick Robert wrote his father about the stone:

I can now give you full tidings of the safety of your great concern here in England. I hope that something will be done in your grand affair by next spring and that I shall be able to have a crystal made of it in its true polite shape. The King of Prussia, if able, is the likeliest chapman at present; though, were peace made, the King of France would certainly be the man. Mr. Cope has the cutting of it. Our present design is a single stone, and we hope to make it a brilliant. It proves the first water, but will be diminished almost one half in cutting. We have so managed it that what is cut off is in great pieces and will sell for a good sum of money. Mr. Cope says that when finished, it will weigh about 280 carats and will be the wonder of the world.

Although agitated by Robert's previous negligence, Governor Pitt read his son's letter and smiled with satisfaction. Color, clarity, cut, and carat size determine a diamond's value. The Governor knew the stone's color and clarity were superb. He approved of the cutter, Mr. Cope, who had a fine reputation. The brilliant shape mentioned in Robert's letter promised to give the stone maximum life. The proposed 280-carat size would guarantee an excellent selling price. For the first time in months, the pressure in Pitt's stomach eased.

The Governor's euphoria passed quickly with one piece of bad news following another. Alvarez refused any further responsibility for the diamond. Pitt wrote Evans: "Tis not a little unkind that Mr. Alvarez refuses me his assistance in the matter."

Possibly rumors of the diamond's illicit origin or difficulties with the stone's tempermental owner caused Alvarez to back off the project. Later, hoping for a slice of the profit, Alvarez relented, assisting in the sale of the chips cut from the diamond.

On December 18th, 1704, Robert again wrote his father:

The cutting of your grand concern licks off a world of money, and I hope that by the next ship you will have made us some remittances. I also hope that the pieces that

will be cut off will greatly help to defray the charge. We
have lately sold three for 2,000 pounds and anticipate
that those to come off will fetch as good a sum. I hope
that when you arrive you will find it finished and the
finest brilliant in the world. The only defect I fear is the
want of a chapman while the war lasts, but the victories
of the Duke of Marlborough last summer give hopes of
a speedy peace.

Robert's letter encouraged the Governor. Imagine the elder
Pitt's dismay when he learned the finished diamond weighed little
more than one-half of Cope's original estimate, and the cost of the
cutting rose to 5,000 pounds. Feeling duped by his son, Evans,
and the cutter, he fired off a letter to Cope on October 12th, 1705:

My son, by your direction, wrote to me in January 1703,
when you had the stone in your hands about eight
months and, as I suppose, had begun to work on it, that
it would make a clean stone, a brilliant of 280 carats, and
the pieces sawed off worth a great sum. Now you tell me
it will be but 140 carats, and the pieces worth little that
are sawed off.

That very day, Pitt also wrote his son Robert:

The disappointment in that grand concern has not a
little disquieted me. I charge that you never permit the
selling of it under 1,500 pounds a carat, and that all my
business be managed with the greatest secrecy imagi-
nable and without ostentation. But I think it is too late
to forbid that, since you have set up to live at the rate I
hear you do, which makes me remember the words of
Osborne, that children are certain trouble but uncertain
comforts.

Prior to receiving his father's testy outburst, Robert wrote on
January 3rd, 1706:

Your grand concern is now almost finished. It is a most
glorious sight, but the outer coat was so foul, and the
flaws went so deep in it, that it will not come net above
140 carats. The reason why the pieces yielded no more
was that they were full of flaws; Mr. Alvarez and Mr.
Cope both think they have been sold for their full value.
When finished the stone will be locked up pending your
arrival or further order.

In an ensuing letter, Robert elaborated:

I find you lay very much to heart the disappointment in
the weight of your grand concern. Mr. Cope, when he
first began to cut it, told me it would come out near 280
carats; when more pieces were taken off, finding it fouler
than he had expected, he told me 180 carats; afterwards
the sawing off of two more pieces reduced it to its present
weight. The stone was entirely perfect in the middle,
and of the best water in the world, but the flaws on the
outside went so deep that it was necessary to saw off all
those pieces, one of the last was so rotten that it crum-
bled into dirt. . . . I cannot imagine that you were in any
ways cheated, for there was never a piece sawed off that I
did not myself put on the place whence it was taken, and
see if it exactly fitted. Mr. Alvarez was the chief manager
in the sale of the pieces, and he protested that he would
not have given so much for them, and that, had they
been his own, he would have sold them for the same
money. It has been finished ever since March last, and
locked up in an iron chest which stands in Sir Stephen's
back shop; he keeps the key of the padlock, and I keep
two keys which unlock the chest.

When Sir Stephen and John Dolben, the Governor's emissary from Fort St. George, corroborated Robert's story, Pitt
resigned himself to the diamond's reduced size. On September
16th, 1707, the Governor wrote his son: "Your letter of January

20 satisfies me entirely as to my grand concern and your disposing of the pieces cut off it."

Had Robert provided an explanation earlier, he might have saved himself and his father the mutual suspicion and animosity that would continue throughout the balance of their lives.

After more than two years' work and a cost exceeding 5,000 pounds, Cope had completed his task. The nearly flawless 140¾-carat stone became the finest large diamond ever cut. Pitt should have felt exhilarated. Instead, his fears intensified. He imagined everyone around him plotted to steal the diamond.

When a rumor of Sir Stephen Evans's impending bankruptcy surfaced, the Governor ordered Robert to retrieve the diamond and transfer it to his cousin George Pitt's home at Strathfieldsaye for safekeeping. Evans reluctantly released the diamond after forcing Robert to sign an agreement promising to pay 5 percent of any future selling price. Robert's prompt action probably saved the diamond from Evans's creditors and protected his father from financial ruin.

At Fort St. George, Pitt's life continued to deteriorate. Although his adversary the Mogul Emperor Aurangzeb died in 1707 at the age of eighty-nine, and the Governor successfully negotiated a treaty with the succeeding ruler, new problems tormented him. The internal bickering with his staff provided a constant irritant. Morbid fears about his diamond's safety ate at him. The infernal Indian heat had begun to sap his strength. Rumors of his wife's infidelity and his son Thomas's prodigal spending tore at his innards. Pitt yearned for the serenity of England.

In a fit of frenzy, he wrote his son Robert on September 22nd, 1706:

> By what I can collect from all my letters, the vileness of your actions on all sides is not to be paralleled in history. Did ever mother, brother, and sisters study one another's ruin and destruction more than my unfortunate and cursed family have done, and I wish you have not had the greatest share in it, for I cannot believe you innocent. This has so distracted my thoughts, staggered my resolutions,

broken my measures, that I know not what to resolve
upon, nor in what part of the world to seek for repose.

With the diamond's safety and family problems pressing in
on him, the Governor's nerves frayed. Quarrels with the members of his council added enemies every day. The illness and
eventual death of his friend and protector in England, Sir Thomas
Cook, and his mishandling of a native outbreak finally presented
the East India Company with the ammunition to recall him.
The directors ordered Governor Pitt home in a letter dated
January 28th, 1709:

> You having for some time past intimated to us your
> desire to return to England, we have granted your request,
> and have appointed Mr. Gulston Addison to be Presi-
> dent and Governor of Fort St. George. . . . and by said
> letter have directed that you do immediately surrender
> the government to the succeeding President, and all
> books, papers, effects and other things belonging to us.

At last, Pitt would be free to oversee the sale of his stone.
However, the stigma of the Pitt Diamond's origin resurfaced to
trouble him. At a meeting held on August 3rd, prior to his
departure from Fort St. George, Captain Seaton, a disgruntled
officer he had cashiered previously, accused the Governor "of
buying a great diamond to the Company's prejudice." When
rumblings of the accusation reached across the seas, the London
newspapers seized the story, alerting all England to the existence of the Pitt Diamond, thus magnifying the potential for
theft.

Thankful to be leaving Seaton's allegation behind him in
India, Pitt boarded the *Heathcote* in October. When he reached
the Cape, the Governor transferred to a Dutch ship "to prevent
a long delay" and to avoid returning home on a ship named for
his bitter enemy. The threat of pirates forced his ship to land at
Bergen, Norway, where the Governor wrote Robert: "Be sure to
let me know who was for seizing my person and effects and the

names of all those who have been doing me good or evil offices with the Company."

By the time Thomas Pitt reached London in the autumn of 1710, the fame of his great diamond had preceded him. The entire country talked about its size and beauty although few actually had viewed it. Lady Wentworth, a member of the nobility, wrote her son: "They say it's as big as an egg; I would have the city of London buy it and make a present of it to put in the Queen's crown."

Yes, selling the diamond to the English government as a gift for Queen Anne seemed an excellent idea to Pitt. Unfortunately, war and political unrest had decimated the English treasury, making such a purchase impossible.

Within a few months of his arrival home Pitt found himself confronted by an affidavit from Dewan Saudatulla Khan demanding the diamond's immediate return to India. The Dewan maintained the stone had been stolen from his master, the Great Mogul, the Emperor of India.

Recognizing the seriousness of the charge, the Governor carefully planned his defense. On May 7th, 1711, Pitt appeared before the directors of the Company to present his case.

"That Captain Seaton's a scoundrel and a villain who has slandered my name. Damn his soul! I'm no thief," Pitt shouted, pointing his finger toward the directors. "You know he forged the affadavit from the Dewan."

When Pitt produced documentation proving he legally purchased the diamond from Jamchund, the directors dropped all charges. The Company immediately dispatched a letter ordering the new Governor of Fort St. George "to prevent every handle the Moors may take to embarrass us." The directors also questioned "how it came to pass that when the diamond had been in England several years before, the natives, if that letter was genuine, never mentioned anything about it till after the late president was come to England."

With his reputation intact but the sale of the great stone stalled, Governor Pitt settled into a large home in London. He maintained an excellent wine cellar and lavishly entertained his political cronies. Active in Parliament, Pitt supported the Whig government. Although his family life proved disastrous, he doted on his youngest daughter, Lucy, a soft and gentle girl who married General James Stanhope, a military hero and staunch member of the Whig party.

When the Governor's plan to sell his diamond to Queen Anne failed, he showed the stone throughout Europe whenever a likely buyer surfaced. On August 1st of 1714, Queen Anne died. Using his political influence, the Governor arranged an appointment to show the diamond to the future ruler of England, King George. On October 2nd, Thomas Pitt wrote:

> I was this day above an hour with the King and Prince. Certainly their aspect promises prosperity to the country. I showed them the great diamond, which they admired and seemed desirous of it, but I believe, hope the nation will give.

War had sapped the country's resources. The English armies were occupied in Flanders, and the Exchequer had more pressing needs. England could ill-afford such a luxury. Pitt recognized George would never purchase the diamond. With each day's disappointment, the Governor's regret concerning his stone grew. Although many admired his treasure, the diamond lacked a serious buyer. Fifteen years had passed since he had purchased the stone from Jamchund. During the ensuing years, rumors had darkened his reputation. His family life had suffered so terribly he barely spoke to his eldest son.

The Governor had distributed models of the diamond to the kings of France, Spain and Prussia to no avail. The prospects for a sale looked remote. The diamond had drained his finances. The Governor's disposition soured with each setback, and he snapped at his family at the slightest provocation.[10]

Just when matters seemed the bleakest, Governor Pitt received an overture from the French crown. Louis XIV, the Sun King, had died on September 1st, 1715. Phillipe, the Duke of Orleans and nephew of the late king, became Regent of France during the minority of Louis XIV's five-year-old great grandson, the future King Louis XV.

Although Phillipe earned notoriety as a womanizer and

drinker, and deservedly so, he proved a capable Regent. The
noted biographer of his age, the Duke of Saint-Simon, described
the forty-one-year-old Regnt:

> ...as of only ordinary tallness at most, quite fleshy
> without being fat; he had an easy expression and way of
> carrying himself; his face was wide, pleasant, quite ruddy,
> his hair black.... His face, his gestures, all his manners
> were imbued with the most perfect graciousness, and it
> came to him so naturally that it adorned even the least
> and most common of his actions.... He was kind, open,
> welcoming, easily accesible and charming, with a pleas-
> ant tone of voice and a gift for words which was particu-
> lar to him.... Few princes have been given a worse
> reputation; none has deserved it less. This enormously
> talented man was a highly competent chemist, a gifted
> and successful general and, as he began now to demon-
> strate, a daring and effective statesman.

Tutored by the roguish Abbe Duclos as a youth, Phillipe
grew up devoid of sexual restraint. He adored the attractive and
easy women of the court. Forced into an unhappy marriage with
the illegitimate daughter of his uncle Louis XIV, he found joy
in a succession of mistresses. Indulging his sexual proclivities to
the fullest, he fathered numerous bastard children. Nonetheless,
his primary concern involved the young king and a cure for the
country's grave financial problems.

When Phillipe first viewed a model of the Pitt Diamond, his
eyes sparkled with desire. He loved fine jewelry. He realized
how wonderful it would be for France to possess such a treasure,
but the price appeared steep. Louis XIV's extravagance had
stretched the treasury to the limit. The costs of the recent War of
the Spanish Succession had left the state virtually bankrupt.

Although Phillipe's heart yearned for the Pitt Diamond, his
mind reminded him of France's financial woes. He refused to
consider the purchase of so great a luxury.

At that time two extremely dissimilar men played an important part in Phillipe's life. The first, John Law, a Scottish outcast born in 1671, left the British Isles after killing a man in a duel. Lean and unattractive, he stood more than six feet tall. However, Law's pock-marked face masked a brilliant mind. In Brussels and Amsterdam, he mastered the secrets of banking. When Law emigrated to France and communicated his vision of paper currency to the government, Phillipe, in his capacity as Regent, allowed him to establish a national bank in 1716.

The bank prospered. Law's financial legerdemain saved France from the brink of bankruptcy. As the economy flourished, the mood of the country improved. Law reduced taxes, abolished duties and brought artisans from abroad to establish new industries. Paris began to import Italian statuary, tapestries from Belgium, paintings and precious jewels.

When Law encountered the model of the Pitt Diamond, he instantly recognized its beauty, but, more importantly, he understood the stone's symbolic significance. He believed the world's most important country deserved such a prize. The hint of a 5,000-pound bribe further whetted Law's appetite for the stone.

Although Law possessed enormous influence, he asked the pompous Duke of Saint-Simon, a confidant to the Regent, for his assistance. The Duke readily agreed to intercede. Saint-Simon wrote in his memoirs:

> Law, who had in many things much grandeur of senti-
> ment, came dispirited to me, bringing the model. I
> thought with him that it was inconsistant with the great-
> ness of a King of France to be repelled from the pur-
> chase of an inestimable jewel, unique of its kind in the
> world, by the mere consideration of price. . . . Law begged
> me to speak to the Duke of Orleans. The state of the
> finances was an obstacle upon which the Regent much
> insisted. He feared blame for making so considerable a
> purchase while the most pressing necessities could only
> be provided with difficulty. I praised this sentiment, but
> I said he ought not to regard the greatest King of Europe
> as he would a private gentlemen, who would be repre-

hensible if he threw away 100,000 livres upon a fine diamond, while he owed many debts which he could not pay. He must consider the honor of the crown and not lose the occasion of obtaining a priceless diamond which would efface the luster of all others in Europe: that it was a glory for his Regency which would last forever; that whatever might be the state of the finances the saving obtained by a refusal of the jewel would not relieve them, for it would be scarcely perceptible; in fact, I did not quit the Duke of Orleans until he had promised that the diamond should be bought.

Thus, the Duke induced Phillipe, the Regent of France, to purchase the Pitt Diamond. After protracted negotiations, the French government agreed to pay 2,000,000 livres, or 125,000 pounds, for the stone, a sum exceeding $600,000 today. The French paid Pitt 40,000 pounds as a downpayment. Pitt agreed to deliver the diamond to Callais for examination by Laurent Rondet, the French crown jeweler. If Rondet approved, the balance of the 85,000 pounds would be paid in four equal installments every six months with 5 percent interest added. As collateral, Rondet would give the Governor four parcels of gems from the Crown Jewels, one parcel to be returned to the French with each payment.[11]

After safely depositing his earnest money in a London bank, the Governor departed for Calais, accompanied by his son-in-law, Charles Cholmondeley, and two of his sons, Thomas, a colonel in the Dragoons, and John, a captain in the Guards.

A concern for the diamond's safety had plagued Pitt from the first moment he owned it. Each day presented new worries to gnaw at him. Although he prepared for the trip to Calais in absolute secrecy, he feared rumors of his mission had escaped.

Villains and thieves frequented the roads along his way. What chance would he and his small band have against a gang of cutthroats? A terrible uneasiness gripped Pitt as he stopped to spend the night at Canterbury, where his son Thomas's regiment was quartered. There, Pitt received a terrible fright related by Sir Henry Yule in his *Documentary Contributions to a Biography of Governor Pitt:*

> Governor Pitt having engaged to deliver his diamond in Calais.... on his way dining at the Crown Inn in Canterbury, called up the landlord, Mr. Lacy, a man of address, who had been consul at Lisbon, and told him that when he traveled he always carried his own wine, not being able to meet with such on the road, and desired him to taste it and give his opinion. Lacy did so and gave it due commendation wishing politely that he could have treated his guest with as good. Upon this Mr. Pitt made him repeat his draught, and at length was so pleased with his frankness as to tell him that he liked him much and wished it was in his power to serve him.

Since the newspapers already had reported the existence of the Pitt diamond, and the Governor appeared in such jovial spirits, the landlord "innocently replied that Pitt had a pebble in his possession which might do him the utmost service."

The landlord laughed at his jest without suspecting the diamond's actual whereabouts or the Governor's nervous state of mind. Pitt's face reddened with anger. Thinking the landlord knew he had the diamond in his possession, Pitt "flew into a violent rage, abusing poor Lacy in the grossest terms (so that he ran frightened out of the room) and saying he should be murdered. In vain did his son and the officers endeavor to pacify him."

After several minutes, the Governor ceased his ranting and became somewhat coherent.

"That fool almost gave me a heart attack! I've settled down now, but I'll not move from this spot without proper protection."

The Governor folded his arms over his chest, insisting an armed guard be stationed by his door for the night. In the morning, he demanded an escort to Dover. Two officers accompanied his band across the Strait of Dover to Calais in France.

At Calais, Pitt and his sons met Rondet in a private room at a roadhouse. The Governor bowed slightly as he presented the diamond to the Frenchman.

"Sir, here is the diamond," said Pitt.

"*Merci,*" Rondet answered, taking the stone in his hand.

Without further amenities, the jeweler scrutinized the diamond. Turning it from side to side, he thought he noticed a small flaw, a fault that would reduce the selling price drastically.

"*Mon Dieu!*" Rondet exclaimed as he rotated the stone between his thumb and forefinger, "what is this I see?"

Instantly sizing up the gravity of Rondet's outburst, John thrust a banknote in the jeweler's hand and urged him to go by the window to examine the diamond in a better light. After a second and more thorough examination, the jeweler pronounced the Pitt Diamond to be perfect, and the sale was consummated.

Although Pitt never received the balance of the purchase price from the French government, the 40,000 pound downpayment and the profit from the sale of the four parcels of Crown Jewels made him one of the wealthiest men in England. The Pitt fortune would one day help his grandson become Prime Minister of England and the city of Pittsburgh to be named in his family's honor.

For over a decade, the Governor had struggled to sell the diamond. At last, he had succeeded, but to his amazement the victory seemed hollow. He had refused the governorship of Jamaica, a prestigious political plum, to give himself time to finalize the sale. When he returned to London on June 29th, 1717, he found few challenges left. The most exciting years of his life had been spent in India. As a man of action, Pitt approached the boredom of retirement with regret.

Although Pitt never again would see the diamond, the stone haunted him one last time. In 1719, the executors of Sir Stephen Evans, the jeweler who assisted in the cutting of the diamond, sued Governor Pitt at Chancery for 5 percent of the purchase price. Years earlier, Pitt's son Robert agreed to pay this commission to induce Evans to release the diamond prior to the jeweler's impending bankruptcy. Even though Pitt never received the full purchase price in cash, the courts forced him to pay the percentage on the total amount.

Pitt's final years brought spiritual and physical pain. His relationship with his wife had ended years earlier after he accused her of infidelity. He barely tolerated his sons Robert and Thomas and detested John. He loved his youngest daughter, Lucy, and her husband, Sir James Stanhope. However, the untimely death of Sir James from a stroke in 1720 proved a terrible blow to Pitt. Lucy's death a few months later crushed the old man.

His robust health faded rapidly. With his will to live weakened, Pitt's once square jaw sagged with age, and his expressive face grew infirm. His palsied fingers bitterly wrote: "The misfortunes that all my sons brought upon me I believe will very soon carry my grey hairs to the grave, and I care not how soon it is, for that I am surrounded with plagues and troubles of the world."

When he prepared his last will, he selected two cousins and his only surviving son-in-law, Charles Cholmondeley, as trustees rather than his sons. On May 21st, 1726, Governor Thomas Pitt, a bitter old man, died of apoplexy.

Bold and shrewd himself, Pitt lacked forbearance for those without his gifts, including his own children. Although he displayed great courage and strength of purpose, Pitt had an innate meanness that continually surfaced.

Governor Pitt's will became his final revenge on his family. John received nothing, Thomas a mere 200 pounds, and, reluctantly, the Governor left Robert the bulk of his wealth. John, Thomas, and Mrs. Pitt each sued Robert for a larger share. The family's battle over the Governor's estate would linger in the courts for years to follow.

FOUR

"C'EST MAGNIFIQUE!" proclaimed Phillipe, the Regent of France, pressing the diamond between his pudgy fingers. His one good eye glowed with pleasure as the light danced across the stone's facets. "My friend Law understood diamonds well. This treasure must be kept in the vault under the care of the minister of finance until our future king comes of age."

Phillipe, the Duke of Orleans, the puffy-cheeked, forty-three-year-old defacto ruler of France, combined the artistic temperment of a Renaissance prince with the morals of a common alley cat. He reveled in debauchery. His wild parties took place behind locked doors guarded by scores of servants. While magic lanterns silhouetted pornographic images on the walls, nude dancers from the opera gyrated to the beat of music.

"Poor Phillipe," mourned the Regent's mother. "The fairies were all invited to the birth of my son. Each one endowed him with some happy quality, but one wicked fairy who had been forgotten came likewise, leaning upon her stick, and not being able to annul her sisters' gifts, declared that the prince should never know how to use them. Alas, the fairy's curse proved true."

During the early years of the Regency, Phillipe relied on John Law and the Duke of Saint-Simon for advice. Law, the financial genius who had engineered the purchase of the Pitt Diamond, now renamed the Regent in Phillipe's honor, became France's newest celebrity. His ideas glowed as brightly as the diamond. Law realized the flow of money nourished the economy.

His bank flooded the country with paper currency. In 1717, the visionary Scotsman unleashed a scheme investing in the new Mississippi territory. Publicity posters depicted French explorers admiring mountains of gold while the copy explained how the Indians of the new world gladly exchanged valuable metal for mere baubles. Noblemen, farmers, soldiers and bourgeoisie all speculated wildly. By 1719, the investors grew rich. By 1720, the Mississippi bubble burst, and Law had been forced to flee from France. The newspapers satirized the sentiments of the angry investors:

On Monday, I bought share on share;
On Tuesday, I was a millionaire;
On Wednesday, took a grand abode;
On Thursday, in my carriage rode;
On Friday, drove to the opera ball;
On Saturday, came to pauper's hall.

The Regent's mother stated only two people ever understood Law's monetary system, the King of Sicily and her son, Phillipe. The King of Sicily rejected Law's economic proposals, insisting he lacked power enough to risk ruination. Unfortunately, Phillipe gambled and lost. On March 21st, 1729, John Law died a pauper in Venice.

As to the Duke of Saint-Simon, his incessant preaching irritated the fun-loving Regent. Shortly after appointing the Duke ambassador to Spain in 1721, Phillipe ostracized him from court.[12]

The years of late nights and drinking ruined Phillipe's health. On December 2nd, 1723, wearied from the day's activities, Phillipe eased into an armchair seated by the hearth. His body ached strangely. His blond-haired mistress, Madame de Falares, knelt by his chair. A hot fire crackled, banishing the chill of winter from the room. Yet, his legs felt strangely cold.

"Do you believe in good faith that there is a God, a hell and a paradise after life?" Phillipe asked.

"Yes, My Prince, I believe it utterly," his mistress answered.

"If what you say is true, you must be very unhappy about the life you are leading."

"I hope God will forgive me," replied Madame de Falares.

Phillipe swallowed a drop of cinnamon-flavored liquor from his glass, sighed and slumped forward in his chair, dead of apoplexy at the age of forty-nine.

With Phillipe gone, the young King Louis XV now would rule all France without family support. Louis had been a beautiful child with liquid black eyes and a handsome Bourbon nose. However, a streak of cruelty blotted his character. As a boy, he tortured three kittens to death. When a noble complained of an ache in his foot caused by gout, young Louis stomped on the man's foot.

As he grew into adolescence, Louis learned to curb his temper. His uncle, the Regent, had taught him a king who is feared by his subjects instead of serving as their defender is more unhappy than the vilest of beasts. Louis vowed to play his role as a ruler well.

Louis first wore the Regent Diamond on March 21st, 1721, while receiving a delegation from Turkey. Dressed in a red velour suit with diamond buttons which once belonged to his great-grandfather Louis XIV, the eleven-year-old child sat with quiet dignity on a stiff-backed chair. The Regent Diamond set in a pearl and diamond knot glistened from his shoulder dazzling the Ottoman ambassador, who commented on its perfect size and shape. The boy's hat contained the Sancy Diamond placed in a clasp. In March of the following year, Louis wore the Regent and Sancy diamonds to a *Te Deum* mass held at Notre Dame Cathedral to celebrate an alliance between France and Spain.

On October 25, 1722, Bishop Fleury crowned the thirteen-year-old Louis XV King of France during a magnificent ceremony at the Gothic cathedral in Reims. Laurent and Claude Rondet, the guardians of the crown jewels, spent many months designing the King's headpiece.

Prior to the coronation, an advertisement in the *Mercure*, one of Paris's leading newspapers, invited the public to view the crown at the Rondets' workshop in the Louvre. A lawyer named Barbier wrote in his diary:

I saw at the workshop of M. Rondet, the jeweler to the King, the crown of Louis XV that was made for the coronation. It was the most perfect work I had ever seen. It was composed of eight branches whose base formed a fleur-de-lis in diamonds and at the top was an isolated fleur-de-lis. A diamond at the top of the fleur-de-lis called the Sancy, which was the most beautiful during the time of Louis XIV, was placed at the top of the fleur-de-lis. In the center of the front, there was the large diamond that the Regent had purchased for the King. It is surprising by its size. It was called the Millionaire when it was worth three million. There is no larger one even at the court of the great Mogul.

The *Mercure* also presented Rondet's official description of the crown as follows:

The circlet or diadem of this superb crown is bordered with two strings of pearls adorned with eight stones of different colors, very large and very perfect, between each of which are three diamonds linked together by very delicate ornaments.

Eight fleur-de-lis of diamonds rise above each of the colored gems on the diadem, and eight fleurons or ornaments, composed each of three stones of various colors, are placed between each fleur-de-lis. The heads of the eight fleur-de-lis are formed of eight table diamonds known as Mazarins, the arms and centers of the three other diamonds and the cross pieces are each a single diamond oblong in shape.

The great and very perfect diamond, known as the Regent, bought for the King by the Duke of Orleans, forms the body and the cross piece of the fleur-de-lis in the front of the crown.

From the eight fleur-de-lis above spring eight branches or arches close to the crown; they are adorned with diamonds and gems of various colors.

A string of pearls with two rows of little brilliants
serves to unite the eight arches and as a base for the
fleur-de-lis terminating the crown.

Between those eight branches and at the spot where
they unite are eight great drop diamonds shaped like so
many springing branches and a kind of sun, if the
crown is regarded from a bird's eye point of view.

This fleur-de-lis, which dominates all others, is isolated.
The head is composed of a pear-shaped diamond named
the Sancy; the cross arms are composed of fifteen diamonds set back to back and joined together by little
ornaments to correspond with the size of the Sancy. The
bonnet is of violet satin, enriched with twenty-five diamonds linked together by very delicate gold embroidery.
This admirable work of art, set a' jour, weighing about
thirty-two ounces was executed under the supervision
and from the designs of M. Rondet's son, associated
with M. Rondet his father in supplying all the gems of
which the King had need.[13]

On September 5th, 1725, at Fontainbleau, Louis XV married
Marie Leczinski, the impoverished daughter of the deposed king
of Poland. The King was fifteen and Marie twenty-two.

Rondet dismounted the stones from the King's coronation
crown for the Queen to wear at the ceremony. He created a
perfectly balanced eight inch-tall, sixteen ounce, vermeil headpiece composed of one hundred and thirty-eight diamonds and
forty pearls. The Regent Diamond ornamented her hair. Gold
clips covered her sleeves. Around her neck she wore the Sancy
Diamond on a necklace called a *carcans* or iron collar. A violet
velour coat encrusted with a gold and diamond fleur-de-lis
added to her elegance. Although most people considered the
Queen plain and dowdy, she radiated the beauty of love on her
wedding day.

Marie wore the Sancy and the Regent on numerous state
occasions. However, the court historians provide few references
concerning the Queen's jewelry. The crown jewelers Rondet and

Son maintained scanty records. In 1752, Piere-André Jacquemin succeeded Rondet as the crown jeweler. When the Duke of Aiguillon replaced Jacquemin in 1773, he complained that history would have been better served if the previous crown jewelers had kept better records.

The inventory of 1774 highlighted some of the decorative pieces Louis and Marie had commissioned. Rondet created a colored stone epaulette, several necklaces, a rope of diamonds and pearls, a pendant and a belt for the Queen while Jacquemin designed a cross featuring the famous blue diamond Jean Baptiste Tavernier had sold to Louis XIV as well as a coat of arms whose center contained a ruby-encrusted dove of peace.

New techniques had revolutionized the manufacturing of jewelry during the early eighteenth century. Jewelers created models of their designs using synthetic stones mounted in wax on a wood base prior to actual execution. Artisans mounted much of the jewelry in open latticework to increase the flow of light. Most pieces contained both colored stones and diamonds for balance, and in some pieces the stones were painted for effect.[14]

Happiness marked Louis and Marie's early years of marriage. Eight girls and two boys blessed the couple in rapid succession between 1727 and 1737. During this time, the King remained faithful to his wife, but with age and maturity, Louis developed stronger sexual desires than his dull and shy wife could provide. The bedroom had always been a tiresome chore for the Queen. As Marie involved herself with reading and prayer, the King found fulfillment elsewhere.

Sometime in 1733, Louis took the Comtesse de Mailly as his mistress. By 1739, the King had tired of the Comtesse, bedding the Marquise de Vintimille, a sister of his former lover. In 1742, Louis took a third sister to his bed, the Duchesse de Chateauroux. The older sisters had been unattractive. The youngest's large blue eyes, long blond hair, and witty spirit gave her a majestic appearance. The King adored the Duchesse, who died of smallpox in 1743 at the age of twenty-seven.

Louis quickly found solace with Madame de Pompadour. He

was thirty-five and she twenty-four. She was slim and graceful, well versed in music and literature. He was tall and handsome, the most powerful king in Europe. Their romance became one of the most famous love affairs of the century.

The poor city dwellers of Paris resented the King's sexual excesses and lack of concern for their hunger. The philosophical discourses of Rousseau, Morilly's espousal of Communism and the growth of Freemasonry added to a spirit of unrest.

At six in the evening, on January 5th, 1757, a valet opened the door to the King's carriage in the snow-covered courtyard at Versailles. Torch-bearing Swiss guards in full costume lit Louis's way as he descended the steps of the palace.

The Grand Equerry assisted the King with the bottom step. Suddenly, a man sprang forth from the shadows, pushing two guards aside and striking the King with a knife.

"Someone has punched me," cried the startled King. Touching his side, he felt the oozing of blood. "I am wounded. Arrest that man, but do not kill him."

The footman, seeing the blood seep through the King's coat, shouted, "The King is wounded." As the guards seized the assassin, attendants tried to carry the King back to his rooms.

"No, I am still strong enough to go up myself," and he walked up the stairs. Back in his room, the blood poured from his side. The King believed himself to be mortally wounded.

A surgeon dressed the wound and gave the King an emetic in case the knife had been poisoned. An old soldier named Landsmath, a huntsman to the King, came to visit his master the next day.

"They got you between your fifth and sixth rib, the doctor says, but you'll be fine, Sire." Landsmath handed the King a chamberpot. "Piss, Sire." There was no trace of blood in the King's urine. "Now, spit in my hand." Again, there was no trace of blood. "I ain't no doctor, but neither your bladder nor lungs have been touched. You'll soon be back at the hunt." In a week the King had recuperated.

The assassin, Robert Damiens, an illiterate forty-two-year-old unemployed servant, suffered a violent death. After days of torture, guards took Damiens to a scaffold at the Place des Greves. The executioner chained his right hand to an iron bar and poured boiling sulphur on it. "You'll not use that hand again to stab our King," snarled the executioner. A second torturer plucked flesh from Damiens' arms with red-hot pincers while a third poured sulphur on the screaming victim's open wounds.

When Damiens lost consciousness, the guards poured water on his face to revive him. As soon as he awakened, the guards tied a horse to each of his limbs. The chief executioner whipped the horses, but Damiens' strong peasant body resisted. The executioner sliced the muscles of the criminal's arms and legs like a butcher cutting meat, and the horses galloped in four different directions with Damiens' parts trailing.

Thereafter, the King always kept a guard near him. His paramour Madame de Pompadour became his unofficial prime minister and best friend until her early death in 1764. In 1765, the King lost his son, the Dauphin, to consumption. Death continued to haunt Louis. In 1768, both his daughter-in-law, the Dauphine, and his patient and long suffering wife died. However, Louis wasted little time in finding a new mistress, the former prostitute Madame du Barry.

In 1770, Louis's sixteen-year-old grandson, Louis-Auguste, the new Dauphin and heir to the throne, married Marie Antoinette, the beautiful fourteen-year-old daughter of Empress Maria Theresa of Austria. Marie's deep blue eyes, auburn hair, and wonderful manners charmed the King. When she innocently asked the function of Madame du Barry, the King's mistress, Louis became so smitten with Marie's naiveté that he toyed with the idea of marrying her himself. However, the Princess could also be spoiled and difficult. Louis later chastised her for snubbing Madame du Barry.

The King had little respect for the new Dauphin. His grandson was good rather than bright, overweight and shy. "Look at that big boy," said Louis, shaking his head in despair. "He will be the ruin of France and of himself, but at least I shall not live to see it."

Louis XV, like his grandfather Louis XIV, outlived his usefulness. As his contemporaries died of old age, the King's body
appeared vigorous. When his lust tired of the young and volup-
tuous Madame du Barry, he bedded teenage girls for variety.
One had been infected with smallpox. On April 17, 1774, the
disease marked his face and body. His head grew red and
swollen. Doctors fed him opium to dull the pain.

On Saturday, May 7th, the King confessed his sins to a priest.
Visions from his earlier years permeated his fever-racked brain.
He recalled the highs and lows of his fifty-nine year reign, from
the glorious moment of his coronation with the Regent Diamond adorning his crown to his near assassination by Damiens
and his present illness. By evening, Louis lapsed into delirium.
The scabs on his face dried and blackened, a sure sign death
would follow. On May 10th, the sixty-four-year-old monarch
died. Aides hurried to bury the stinking corpse in the royal
vaults at Saint-Denis to escape possible contagion.

The King had spent more time with his hounds and the hunt
than with his ministers. He watched while Canada, India, and
Mississippi slipped away from France. Costly wars created a
legacy of poverty for the lower classes and social unrest among
the bourgeoisie. While the poor cried out for food, the middle
class demanded increased power based on talent rather than
title. Few mourned the death of Louis XV, a king remembered
for his sexual proclivities rather than his skill in redressing the
country's problems.

FIVE

A SEA OF FAT smothered young Louis XVI's chin. His bloated face and ponderous belly smacked more of a jester than a king. Clumsy and near-sighted, he plodded through the palace like a lethargic ox. Words emanated from his mouth with difficulty, his hollow and reedy voice dulling their impact. He detested the responsibility of ruling a powerful country, preferring to work with his hands rather than his mind. Louis possessed a good heart but lacked ambition.

On the day his grandfather Louis XV died, Louis XVI accepted the crown with reluctance. When messengers burst through his suite shouting the traditional cry of "The King is dead! Long live the King," the twenty-year-old monarch fell to his knees cowering at his wife's side and sobbed: "Protect us. We are too young to rule." Louis would never mature to the demands of the crown.

Louis XVI sought a simple life. He enjoyed hunting. Each night, he retired to bed by eleven. In contrast, his wife, Marie Antoinette, loved the night. She craved the adulation of the nobility. Opera, theater, the *Comedia Francaise*, masked balls and gaming houses excited her. The Queen's extravagant tastes became legendary.

During the first seven years of marriage and until he underwent a painful operation, the King lacked the capability to consummate sex. He suffered from phimosis, a tightness of the foreskin, making intercourse impossible. Since Louis lacked the ability to satisfy his wife sexually, he compensated by providing her with every possible luxury.

The court at Versailles included 886 noblemen plus wives and children, 295 cooks, 56 hunters, 47 musicians, 8 architects and 6,000 assorted secretaries, chaplains, doctors, maids and servants. An army of 10,000 soldiers remained quartered in the nearby town. The crown spent nearly one tenth of France's total tax revenues to maintain this royal retinue.

The Queen's voracious appetite for personal finery further strained the country's budget. While Monsieur Leonard designed Madame's hair, Madamoiselle Bertin supervised her wardrobe. Diamonds fascinated Marie Antoinette. She opted for jewelry accented with open latticework settings instead of the heavier colored stone and diamond pieces favored by her predecessors. She commissioned the jewelers Charles Boehmer and Paul Bassenge to remove the Regent, Sancy and Mazarin diamonds from the ornamental mountings patterned for the court of Louis XV to create a variety of new and unique designs. For a costume ball, Marie Antoinette, disguising herself as a woman she called the mysterious Gabriel d'Estrees, wore the Regent in an aigrette of white heron's feathers attached to a black hat. On another occasion, she positioned the crown diamonds on a floral brooch set as drops of water on a garland of flowers.

In 1776, the King purchased a pair of magnificent, girandole, pear-shaped drop earrings for the Queen from Boehmer at a cost exceeding $100,000. Six months later, the Queen bought a pair of diamond bracelets at more than $50,000. While she spent another $50,000 on her wardrobe and almost twice as much again on her gambling debts during the year, France teetered on bankruptcy.

The Queen's mother lectured her on frugality:

A Queen only degrades herself by decking herself out in this preposterous way, and she degrades herself even more by unthrifty expenditures, especially in such difficult times. I know too well how extravagant are your tastes, and I cannot keep silent about the matter. Every-

one knows that the King is modest in his expenditure,
so the whole blame will rest on your shoulders. I hope I
shall not see the disaster that is likely to ensue.

People in the streets called their spendthrift Queen "Madame
Deficit." When the Queen attended dances and plays without
the King, rumors of sexual infidelity circulated linking her
name with Count Alex Fersen, a tall and handsome Swede.
Books such as *Les Amours de Charlot et Toinette* accused Marie
Antoinette of having an affair with the King's younger brother,
the Count of Artois. Incensed peasants chanted in the streets:

My little Queen, not twenty-one,
Maltreat the folks, as you've begun,
And o'er the border you shall run.

Failing to heed the admonitions of the peasants and her
mother, the Queen followed the advice of Catherine II of Russia,
who wrote her: "Kings and Queens ought to proceed in their
careers undisturbed by the cries of the people as the moon
pursues her course unimpeded by the howling of dogs."

The publicist Mirabeau described the country's situation
thusly: "From stagnant chaos, France has passed to tumultuous
chaos." The nobility and clergy frustrated the ambitious middle
class. Rising food prices brought the peasants to starvation.
While the King hunted and the Queen danced, France simmered
with revolution.

When Marie's brother, Joseph, visited France in 1777, he
warned the young Queen:

You are getting older, and no longer have youth as an
excuse. What will become of you if you delay any longer
to reform? . . . Have you thought what effect your intima-
cies and friendships must have on the public? I really
tremble for your happiness, for it cannot turn out well
in the long run, and there will be a cruel revolution
unless you take steps against it.

With hostility building daily, an unsavory incident called the Diamond Necklace Affair solidified the country against Marie Antoinette. Several years earlier, the jeweler Boehmer had created an elaborate 2,800-carat diamond collar for Louis XV to present to his mistress Madame du Barry. When Louis XV died before purchasing his gift, Boehmer attempted to sell the necklace to various crown heads of Europe. Unable to locate a buyer anywhere, the jeweler pleaded with Marie Antoinette to purchase the necklace. The Queen declined.

The Queen's refusal should have ended the affair. However, a complex series of events carried the diamond necklace to the forefront of French history. In 1774, Cardinal Rohan, while serving as the French ambassador to Vienna, offended Marie Antoinette's mother, Maria Theresa. When the Cardinal returned to France, Marie Antoinette shunned him. In a letter to her mother, the young Queen wrote: "I believe his principles are very bad and that he is very dangerous on account of his intrigues; if it had depended on me he would have had no post here."

Rohan hoped to regain Marie Antoinette's favor and improve his potential for higher government office by apologizing, but the Queen refused to forgive him. By chance, the Cardinal met a schemer named Countess La Motte, a distant cousin of the King, who convinced Rohan of her influence over Marie Antoinette. The Countess duped the Cardinal into believing he could win the Queen's friendship by assisting in the purchase of a diamond necklace. Rohan readily agreed to help.

On January 24th, 1785, the Countess advised the jewelers Boehmer and Bassange that the Queen would buy their necklace. She explained the sale had to be carried out in the utmost secrecy because the Queen planned to purchase the jewelry without the King's knowledge. An influential person would act as an intermediary to negotiate the terms.

Next, the Countess forged a letter signed "Marie Antoinette of France" and presented it to Rohan as further proof of the Queen's intentions. The Cardinal ignored the fact Marie Antoinette never signed her letters with the name of her country, an obvious clue to the forgery. Rohan showed the letter to the jewelers and arranged a purchase price of 1,600,000 livres, or approximately $350,000, payable in quarterly installments over a two-year period. The Cardinal even advanced a small downpayment to seal the agreement.

On January 30th, the Cardinal visited the home of the noted psychic Cagliostro, who guaranteed him the spirits would smile kindly on the affair. Thus assured, the Cardinal overlooked the flaws in the Countess's story and proceeded to conclude the purchase.

On February 1st, the jewelers presented the necklace to the Cardinal, who in turn gave it to a man he believed to be the Queen's valet. The supposed valet handed the necklace to Countess La Motte. Rohan eagerly awaited a word of pardon from the Queen.

A few months later, Boehmer petitioned the Queen for the first payment. A surprised Marie Antoinette declared she neither had ordered nor received any necklace. A scandal quickly exploded. The King ordered the arrest of Cardinal Rohan. A trial followed, and the judges acquitted Rohan. The court ordered the arrest of Countess La Motte, whose husband previously had smuggled the necklace into England, where it had been broken up and sold. After the police captured the Countess, the judge ordered her to be whipped, branded with a "V" for *voleuse* or thief and imprisoned.

Although La Motte's conviction cleared Marie Antoinette of any wrongdoing, a flood of libel spewed forth spotlighting the Queen's private life. Parisian cafe gossips swore the Queen had orchestrated events to avenge herself on the Cardinal and get the necklace without paying for it. Thus, the Diamond Necklace Affair branded the Queen as a cheat, a swindler and an enemy of the people.

The typical peasant paid nearly one half of his income in taxes while the Queen squandered millions of livres. "Hunger alone will cause this great revolution," prophesied the Marquis Girardin. When the famine of 1788 coupled with the cruel winter of 1789 caused bread to rise from nine sous in August to fourteen in February, the poor demanded food.

Although the people loved the King, Louis's ineffectuality sealed his fate.

On the afternoon of July 12th, 1789, Camille Desmoulins, a twenty-nine-year-old radical lawyer, jumped atop a table outside a cafe near the *Palais-Royal*. Brandishing a pistol in one hand and a sword in the other, he shouted: "To Arms!" Leaping from the table, Desmoulins rushed to the *Place Vendome*, a rabid crowd behind him.

The following day, a hungry mob seized the grain from the Monastery of Saint Lazare. A second and more violent force freed the inmates at the prison of LaForce. On July 14th, more than 8,000 rebels stormed the armory at the *Hotel des Invalides*, capturing 32,000 muskets. A loud voice shouted, "To the Bastille!" Like a baby whose time had come, bursting from its mother's womb into the world outside, the French Revolution exploded with a shriek in a sea of blood.

The Duke of Rochefoucauld awakened the King in his bed chamber and announced: "The Bastille has been taken! The Governor has been murdered. His head on the point of a spike is being carried in triumph through the streets."

"Why this is a revolt," answered the King with characteristic naiveté.

"No, Sire," said the Duke. "It is revolution."

With each ensuing day, the citizenry demanded more power. On October 6th, a mob of starving peasants surged past the guards at Versailles, screaming: "To the Queen's apartments!" The terrified Queen fled to the Bull's Eye Room with her family.

After the mob murdered several soldiers guarding her apartments, a bleeding officer burst into the Queen's quarters, shouting: "Madame, fly for your safety."

"No, Monsieur," answered the Queen. "Nothing will induce me to be separated from my husband. I know that they seek my life, but I am the daughter of Maria Theresa and have learned not to fear death."

The Queen's bravery quieted the mob, and the rioting subsided after the King agreed to return to Paris. Cheering peasants escorted the royal family from Versailles to their new quarters in the Tuileries.

In Paris, the mood of the people soured quickly. The Tuileries became a virtual prison. Louis's younger brothers, the Counts of Provence and Artois, fled to Brussels. Recognizing the danger to her family, Marie Antoinette plotted an escape. She packed her diamonds and jewels in cotton-lined boxes, entrusting them to her hairdresser for delivery to Brussels. When a spy alerted the Assembly, the police captured the hairdresser with the jewels before he could leave the country.

On June 20th, 1791, at eleven in the evening, the royal couple, their two children and the King's sister, Elizabeth, fled the Tuileries in a carriage. In Varennes, a citizen recognized the royal family and had them arrested. Six thousand armed men escorted the royal family back to Paris in a humiliating one-hundred-and-eighty mile, four-day trek.

Following the King's return to Paris, the Committee of Public Safety took steps to insure the future safety of the Crown Jewels. Expert jewelers made a new inventory on June 25th, 1791, valuing the jewels at more than 28,000,000 francs. The *Garde-Meuble*, a furniture repository and museum, became the new home for the Crown Jewels.

The authorities permitted the citizenry of France to visit the *Garde-Meuble* one day per week. People could view collections of armor, state beds, Cardinal Richelieu's church plate and a handsome collection of tapestries, among other treasures. On the first floor in a side room, the Regent Diamond, renamed the National Diamond by the revolutionaries, rested in a glass display case along with other Crown Jewels for all to see.

On June 20th, 1792, Thierry de Ville d'Avray, the curator of the *Garde-Meuble*, sensing the potential for burglary, ordered the Crown Jewels to be removed from the glass cases and hidden in eight separate boxes. He concealed the boxes in an inlaid cabinet whose drawers were secured by heavy copper locks. Thierry congratulated himself on his foresight as he watched the unsavory crowds milling outside the window of the *Garde-Meuble* each day.

Less than a block away, the royal family worried about their safety. Paris was in turmoil. Hordes of desperate revolutionaries and common criminals stood defiantly outside the palace walls. The King rarely spoke, ignoring the unpleasantness surrounding him. The Queen steeled herself to meet whatever fate delivered.

That same June 20th, a mob broke into the Tuileries. In unison, the crowd shouted: "Down with Mr. Veto. Don't let your wife wear the pants." Armed men forced the King to wear the red bonnet of the Jacobins.[16] In an adjacent room, vulgar women screamed obscenities at the Queen while her fourteen-year-old daughter and seven-year-old son clung to her skirts.

When the crowds attacked the Tuileries again on August 10th, Marie bravely seized two pistols and forced them into her husband's reluctant hands.

"Now, Sire, is the time to show yourself, and if we must perish, let us perish with glory."

"Madame," intervened a nobleman, "are you prepared to take upon yourself the responsibility of the death of the King, of yourself, of your children, and all who are here to defend you? All Paris is on the march. Time presses. In a few minutes it will be too late."

The Queen glanced at her terrified daughter and sighed. Her bold front vanished, and her face turned pale.

"You are right," she answered meekly. "Let us go and seek sanctuary from the Assembly." The King, Queen, Elizabeth and the two children escaped down a staircase protected by Swiss guards to seek refuge in the nearby meeting place of the Assembly.

Like a pack of snarling wolves, the mob massacred the remaining Swiss guards. Then, maddened by the sight of blood, they hurled magnificent mirrors and antique furniture from the windows, dashing them onto the streets. Ignorant peasants crushed priceless gold and silver icons to be melted for scrap value. Common thieves filled their pockets with jewels. Others seized the King's private papers.

Although the country had declared war on Austria, the private papers taken from the Tuileries proved Louis secretly had encouraged his brother-in-law, Emperor Leopold, to invade

France. When the evidence reached the Assembly, its members demanded the King and Queen be tried for treason. The Queen wrote her friend Count Fersen: "The King and Queen are in the greatest danger. . . . No one can tell what will happen in the next twenty-four hours. The troop of assassins grows daily."

On August 13th, the Assembly jailed the royal family in the Temple, a decrepit fourteenth century fortress situated near the site of the Bastille. Weeds choked a once beautiful courtyard. Graffiti marred the walls. The chill of hopelessness made the air cold and heavy. The Queen looked tired and old, her once beautiful hair prematurely grey. She turned to her family and sobbed: "My unhappy friends, a woman even more unhappy than yourselves has caused all your misfortunes." Marie Antoinette fell to her knees on the wet floor and burst into tears.

Each day the jailers increased the hardships on the King and Queen. Furniture would be taken from the room without explanation. The Committee of Public Safety removed paper, pencils, scissors, needles and pins. Although they heard rumors of the deaths of their friends, the prisoners received no communications. After almost six weeks in the Temple, the jailers separated the King and Queen.

On September 20th, 1792, Georges-Jacques Danton, a powerful and ugly lawyer of peasant stock, headed the Assembly. Flanked by his assistants, Camille Desmoulins and Fabre d'Eglantine, Danton declared, "We will have no King." Robespierre and Saint-Just of the radical faction called for the death penalty for the King. Jean Paul Marat sat alone in his bodily stench, a sick, cynical and cruel man who understood the meaning of revolution. "The Republic is only a house of cards until the head of the tyrant falls under the axe of the law!" Marat shouted. He too would vote for Louis XVI's death.

On December 26, 1792, Louis XVI appeared before the revolutionary tribunal with a four-day growth of beard. His ashen complexion and pouchy eyes belied his thirty-eight years. A beaten man, he refused to acknowledge letters written in his own handwriting. On January 20th, by a slim vote, the tribunal sentenced Louis to death.

The following morning a closed carriage conveyed Louis XVI, accompanied by his confessor, to the Place of the Revolution, today known as the *Place de la Concorde*. Dressed in a black coat and matching top hat, the chief executioner, Charles-Henri Sanson, the man who had supervised the quartering of Louis XV's attempted assassin Damiens thirty-four years earlier, led the King to the guillotine.

As the executioner sought to tie Louis's hands, the King resisted. "I will never submit to that. Do your business, but you shall not bind me."

The executioner called for help, but the confessor interceded. "Sire, submit unresistingly to this fresh outrage, as the last resemblance to the Savior who is about to recompense your sufferings." Louis nodded obediently and placed his hands for the executioner to tie.

"Do as you will; I will drink the cup to the dregs," Louis said. Looking first at the blade and then toward the crowd, Louis spoke in a broken voice: "People, I die innocent of all the crimes laid to my charge." The executioner interrupted his speech, forcing him to kneel before the guillotine, his head positioned for impact. "I pardon the authors of my death and pray God that the blood you are about to shed may never fall again upon France. And you unhappy people...." The deafening roar of the drums silenced his last words. The guillotine fell, and the executioner's assistant lifted the King's head from a basket for all to see.

Marie Antoinette suffered gravely following her husband's death. After the Committee of Public Safety accused her of conspiracy, they separated the Queen from her son. The eight-year-old child known as Louis XVII, frantically cried in terror, "O, Mother! Mother! Do not abandon me to these men. They will kill me as they did Papa."

During this difficult time, France operated under a nine-member Committee of Public Safety under Danton's leadership. Following Louis's execution, the Revolution grew increasingly ugly. The terrorists began to feed upon one another. Charlotte Corday murdered Marat with a kitchen knife in his bath on July

13th to protest the massive amount of killings. The pock-marked
Danton, far less brutal than his features suggested, recognized
the violence had gone too far.

"The Seine is running red with blood. Oh, there's too much
blood being shed," Danton wrote.

In early August of 1793, guards awakened the Queen at
midnight, taking her to the Conciergerie, the prison where the
doomed awaited execution. Two armed men led her down slip-
pery stairs to a dark cell. Water oozed along the walls. A tiny
table, a chair and a filthy pallet in the corner of the room were
her only furnishings.

That night she slept fitfully, tears pouring down her face. She
tried to shut out the horror of her surroundings by pretending
she was a young bride dressed in diamonds and jewels, but the
reality of her fate was too strong for her to battle. She wrote a
letter of farewell addressed to her sister-in-law, Elizabeth, asking
her "never to seek to avenge my death."

On the morning of October 16th, 1793, representatives of
the revolutionary government bound the thirty-eight-year-old
Queen's hands behind her back and cut off her hair at the neck.
Like a fly paralyzed by the spider's bite, the Queen patiently
submitted to the humiliating preparation referred to as *"la toilette."*
Soldiers loaded Marie Antoinette aboard a plain horse-driven
cart to meet the guillotine at the Place of the Revolution. A
hush stilled the crowds as the executioner helped the Queen
from the cart. At twelve in the afternoon, executioner Charles-
Henri Sanson held up the Queen's severed head for all to see.

Governor Thomas Pitt

Napoleon Bonaparte wearing the Consular Sword
Painting by Grog

King Louis XV of France

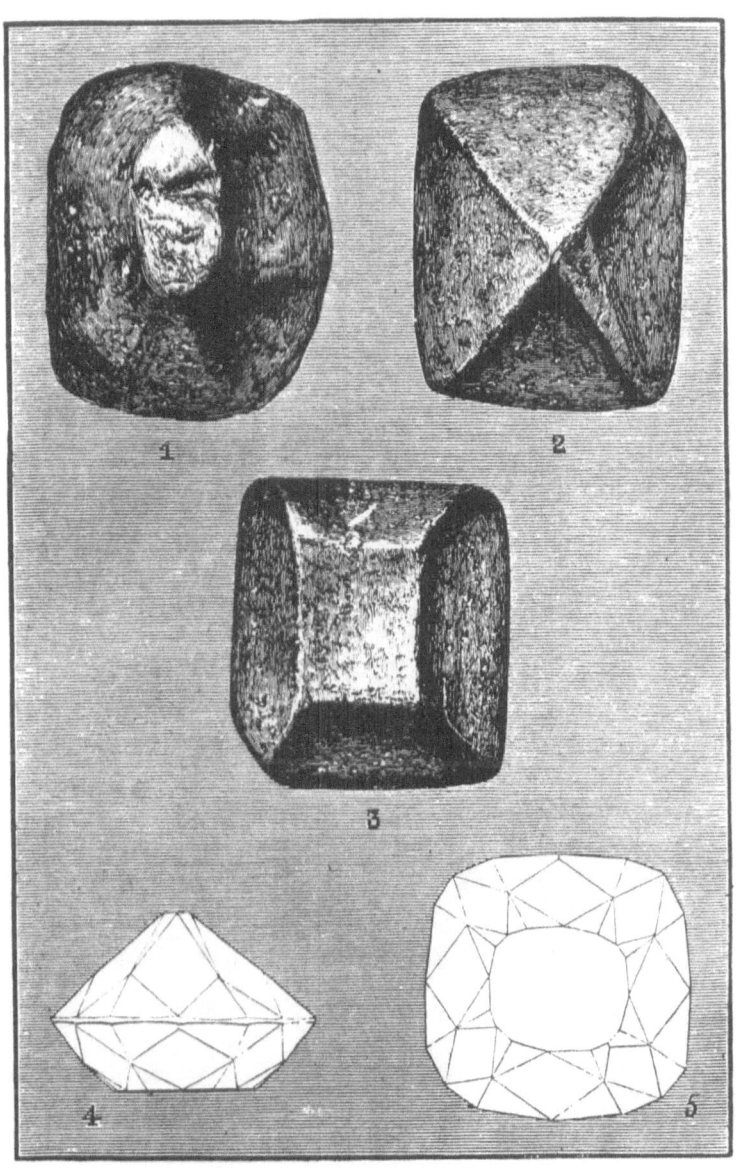

*The Pitt (Regent Diamond): (1) in the rough,
(2 and 3) in successive stages of cutting, and
(4 and 5) as cut.*

The Regent Diamond—140¾ carats

Napoleon Bonaparte's Consular Sword containing the Regent.
Drawing by Lucia Shood

Crown of Louis XV containing the Regent Diamond

Crown of Charles X containing the Regent Diamond.
Drawing by Patrick McCormick

*Necklace from the Queen's Necklace Affair
leading to the French Revolution.*

Meander Tiara of Empress Eugenie containing the Regent.

Empress Eugenie
Drawings by Lucia Shood

Château de Chambord

Fireplace in which the Regent was hidden during World War II.

Galerie d'Appolon at the Louvre Museum

Vitrine containing Regent Diamond.
Photograph by Michele Perelman

SIX

"I SPIT UPON THE REVOLUTION. What has it done to fill my pockets? I rot in this hell-hole of a jail while others are free on the streets," the thief Paul Miette complained to his cellmates at LaForce Prison several months prior to King Louis XVI's execution. "They have robbed me of my freedom, but I have my dreams. My mouth waters when I think about the Crown Jewels in that museum they call the *Garde-Meuble*. I can taste the good life them jewels would bring. Imagine diamonds, rubies and pearls as big as your fist sitting inside glass cases begging to be plucked by them with the mettle to do it? The gold and silver sitting around the room got Paul Miette's name written all over it.

"There's carpets, swords and goblets, but just give me the jewelry. The big square diamond they call the Regent would do fine," Miette snickered.

"The *Garde-Meuble* is watched by soldiers," chimed in one of the prisoners. "It ain't as easy as you make it sound, Paul."

"The pot's ripe for the picking," Miette answered. "The first Tuesday of every month, any Frenchman can visit the building. I've been inside the *Garde-Meuble* more than once. The upper rooms have furniture and arms, but the side room on the first floor holds the real prize, the Regent Diamond. There's guards enough during the day, but at night, only a couple outside. Them fellows are more interested in brandy than protecting the jewels." Miette tapped his questioning comrade on the chest to emphasize his point. "You listen to me. As soon as I get out of

74

this joint, I'm going for the *Garde-Meuble*, and there's more than enough for all of us if you got the stomach to join me."

"Just say the word, and we're with you, Miette," said a young prisoner.

"Sounds good to me, Paul," answered another prisoner. Paul Miette knew he would rob the *Garde-Meuble* some day.

During Miette's imprisonment, on August 16th, 1792, the French Minister of the Interior Cambon proposed selling the Crown Jewels, including the Regent Diamond, to raise funds and prop up the newly issued paper currency. The previous year, the Crown Jewels had been valued at more than 30,000,000 francs. The cash derived from the sale of the jewels could stabilize the country's floundering economy.

While the National Assembly debated the merit of selling the Crown Jewels, the thirty-five-year-old Paul Miette, a perennial felon, fine-tuned his plan to burglarize the *Garde-Meuble*. Miette, a native Parisian, had been arrested in 1779 and again in 1781 for theft. Banished from Paris for nine years by the authorities, he returned in January of 1790 only to be imprisoned for another burglary. After his release the police rearrested him for theft, incarcerating him at LaForce in March of 1792. The crafty Miette would not remain in prison for long.

France boiled with turmoil in the late summer of 1792. The Jacobins demanded the death penalty for the King and Queen. Toughs brutalized the old and the weak with impunity. When the outmanned police force proved incapable of protecting Paris from the rabble, Thierry, the curator of the *Garde-Meuble*, warned the authorities of the potential for the theft of the Crown Jewels. The National Assembly ignored Thierry's request for additional security.

Riot followed riot, culminating in the September 2nd and 3rd massacres in which hundreds of innocent people died. The crazed mob murdered Thierry de Ville along with helpless women, children and clergy. Next, this army of scum burst into the prisons, killing the guards and releasing hundreds of hardened criminals, including Paul Miette. Free at last, Miette called together his band of criminals.

Tricot, Roudany, Basile, Young Guillot, Letort, Delcampo, Delors, Barraud and Constantin, all recently at LaForce, listened intently to Miette's scheme to steal the Crown Jewels.

The *Garde-Meuble* had been erected in 1760 under the supervision of the architect Gabriel. The building stood in the heart of the city near the naval offices and the Tuileries. The main entrance faced Place Louis XV, today called the *Place de la Concorde*. A handsome statue of Louis XV, sculpted by Bouchardon, decorated the front of the *Garde-Meuble*. A second door fronted Saint Florentin across from the Hotel Talleyrand.

The area around Place Louis XV attracted the worst elements of Paris. Thieves, prostitutes and assassins gravitated to the front entrance of the *Garde-Meuble*. The National Guard patrolled the area with frequency during the day to discourage lawlessness. However, the evening of September 11th, 1792, the Guard withdrew without replacements. Since the National Guard had disappeared on previous occasions, the authorities saw little reason for alarm. In fact, the new Minister of the Interior, Roland, jokingly remarked the departure of the National Guard might prevent fires caused by the carelessness of any drunken soldiers.

Following the riots, the Paris Commune closed the *Garde-Meuble* to public visitation. Representatives sealed the commodes protecting the crown, sceptre, coronation ornaments and the more valuable loose stones including the Regent. However, the building itself offered little security against burglary.

While Miette's gang of desperados staked out the *Garde-Meuble*, a second group of criminals from Rouen independently plotted to steal the jewels. The criminals Chapeaurond, Gobert, Cornu, Leconte, Badarel, Cottet, Gallois, Meyran and Groscul banded together under the leadership of a man named Francisque.

On September 11th, at eleven in the evening, the two gangs joined forces in front of the *Garde-Meuble* at the Place Louis XV. One of the thinnest of Francisque's band climbed a colonnade beside the building. Grasping a shutter directly above the colonnade, the thief pried it open to squeeze inside the *Garde-*

Meuble. Luckily for the criminals, the museum guards had failed to secure the protective iron bars designed to cover the shutter. After forcing entry, the thief unlatched a window to permit his confederates to enter.

The burglars worked quietly, fearing unnecessary noise might draw the National Guard. The more experienced men used picks to break into the vitrines, the glass cases containing mounted jewels for public exhibition. Francisque and Paul Miette forced open drawers and emptied their contents. Gobert and Cadet Guillot seized a necklace, golden shoe buckles, a sword, two watches and a pearl in a golden box inscribed "The Queen of Pearls." Gallois and Badarel stood by with candles to light the room.

"Damn! Where is it?" Miette swore. He rummaged through a vitrine of small diamonds searching for the Regent. He sliced his finger on a fragment of glass. Blood oozed from the open wound. "Damn! It ain't here," Miette exclaimed, pounding his other fist on a nearby table.

"Easy Paul, you'll bring the police if you don't shut up. We've got more than enough. Let's get out of here," a second thief warned Miette.

"Guess you're right. Let's go," Miette answered, shrugging his shoulders in agreement.

After cleaning out the cases including the Blue Diamond and the *Cote-de-Bretagne* ruby, the criminals placed an official seal on the doors to discourage anyone from entering the jewel room. Their work completed, the thieves descended through the window just as they had entered. The two groups dispersed into smaller bands to divide the spoils. By two o'clock in the morning, the thieves returned to their respective homes satisfied with the night's take and hopeful of returning another time for more. In actuality, they had missed the greatest prize of all, the marquetry commode containing the Regent, Sancy and Mirror of Portugal Diamonds.

During the night of September 12th, several of the thieves spent the evening drinking at a cabaret on *Fosses-Saint-Germain-l'Auxerrois* bragging about their gains from the *Garde-Meuble*.

"I'd like to return for another dose of medicine," joked a twenty-year-old man.

"That would cure my ache," answered his friend. The second man winked and placed his purse on the table. The two men roared with laughter.

The following evening, the thieves regrouped in even greater numbers under Francisque's leadership. Finding the outside window still open, the burglars entered undetected. Inside the gallery, several lit candles to provide adequate illumination. After going down the steps to the jewel room on the first floor, the thieves broke open the protective locks on the commode, snatching the Crown Jewels.

"Good God!" gasped one thief. "What a treasure."

"Do you see this one?" said another lifting the Regent. The light from the candles made the diamond radiate with an explosion of brilliant reds and greens. With the riches of the French monarchy in their grasp, the thieves stealthily left through the window.

The robbers rested on September 14th, returning again on the 15th. Emboldened by their success, the criminals roamed the *Garde-Meuble* at will, seizing everything of value. While drinking wine and gnawing on cold chicken, they strewed empty bottles and half-eaten bones across the floor.

As the drunken thieves burst onto the street, two men quarreled over the spoils. One sold a box of diamonds to a passerby on the banks of the Seine River at a bargain price. The purchaser took the diamonds to a jeweler, who became suspicious and reported the purchase to the police. When the police checked the *Garde-Meuble,* they found the doors closed and locked. Since everything appeared in order, the authorities dismissed any possibility of theft.

On September 16th, the crime took on the look of a full-scale expedition. Almost fifty people, most released from the prisons during the September massacres, several of them women, entered the building. A few, disguising themselves in the uniforms of the National Guard, blatantly sang the *Carmagnole,* the revolutionary anthem. During this final foray, the robbers seized the remaining treasure, including the jewelry and icons from Cardinal Richelieu's chapel. The greedier among them fought for the spoils like a pack of hungry wolves circling the carcass of their dead prey, ready to strike at one another over the least provocation. Vandals needlessly destroyed priceless tapestries and delicate furnishings too heavy to carry.

This final night of pillaging ended around eleven o'clock. The criminals began their descent down the colonnade to the street. Two latecomers believing themselves to be shorted by their compatriots demanded an immediate split of the spoils from Francisque. The screams from their ensuing argument drew the National Guard to the Place Louis XV.

"Halt!" ordered an officer named Camus. As the thieves scattered, Camus seized a man called Chabert by the arm. At the same instant, a second criminal named Douligny dropped from the lamp post in front of the *Garde-Meuble* only to be surprised by the firm grasp of another guardsman.

"We didn't do nothing," Chabert protested. "Let go of me!"

"Keep hold of them," countered Camus.

Instantaneously concluding the *Garde-Meuble* had been burglarized, Camus tried the door to the building along the interior steps. The locks appeared intact. The officer then assumed the thieves had entered by other means. He ordered ladders placed on the exterior walls of the building. Climbing to the broken shutter, he followed the same route the thieves had.

Camus used a rope as a guide to ease onto a ledge, where he discovered a gold vase given by the City of Paris to commemorate the birth of Louis XV's son. Returning to the building, he saw diamonds cast across the floor among chicken bones and empty wine bottles. A superb pearl lay beside an iron chisel and a lock pick used to break into the vitrines. Unbelievably, neither the curator nor the guards had visited the *Garde-Meuble* during the week of the thefts.

After eyeing the broken seals on the commode and the scattered gems on the floor, Camus returned to the street to question Douligny, who refused to co-operate. Around midnight, Camus locked up the suspects and reported the theft to his superior at

Saint Florentin. Shortly thereafter, the police notified Sargeant, Thierry's successor as the chief of the *Garde-Meuble.*

During further questioning at the station, the twenty-six-year-old Chabert declared his true name to be Jean-Jacques Chambon. In Chambon's pocket the police found a diamond cross and a golden Bachus on horseback on an agate band. Douligny had a diamond and coral rattle given to Louis XVI by Empress Catherine of Russia. Both thieves held unmounted diamonds in their pockets along with burglary tools.

At noon the following day, Camus called in Justice of the Peace Fantin and a stenographer to record Douligny and Chambon's statements.

"I was passing through Place Louis XV after a few drinks when two men invited me to come with them," the twenty-three-year-old Italian born ex-convict Douligny explained. "One of the men climbed a lamp post by the *Garde-Meuble,* and the other followed. What could I do? I thought they had women in the building, so I joined them. When they put jewels in my pockets, I kept them. Wouldn't you? Since I was drunk, I can recall little else."

Chambon told the police some soldiers had apprehended him at eleven o'clock the previous night when he came out of Rue Royale, forcing him to look for some coins on Saint Florentin Street.[17]

The National Guard also had arrested a drunken thief named Badarel at the foot of the statue of Louis XV on the same night that Douligny and Chambon were arrested. A soldier took Badarel to the Conciergerie to await questioning.

The National Convention ordered the Mayor of Paris, Petion, and the Minister of the Interior, Roland, to head the investigation of the theft of the *Garde-Meuble.* Within days other arrests followed. The counterfeiter Lamy-Evette known as Briere, Boutet, Cottet, nicknamed the Little Hunter, Matelot, whose real name was Gallois, Alexander the Little Cardinal and Picard implicated one another in the crime under questioning.

During the first days of hearings, the courts assumed the burglary had been part of a larger political conspiracy. Danton's secretary, Fabre d'Eglantine, accused the Girondins, the conservative arm of the revolutionary government. The radical Marat blamed the aristocrats of attempting to overthrow the revolutionary government. The Public Accuser believed Marie Antoinette and the royalists had masterminded the theft.

"Have you been hired by people of distinction, princes or other noted persons?" the President of the Tribunal asked Douligny.

"No, sir," answered the accused, a common thief rather than a political activist. "I did it for the money."

After initially denying complicity in the theft, Douligny confessed. He implicated a band of prostitutes and thieves who had joined in the crime. Douligny explained to the police he had met the Spaniard Roudani at the Prison of LaForce. He claimed the Spaniard had forced him to take part. Marian, Delange, Delcampo, Paul Miette, Deslors, Lemaitre, Agard, Colin, Fratin, Berequin and Basile had entered the *Garde-Meuble* with him. The Convention immediately placed arrest warrants for those named by Douligny.

On Monday, September 24th, the previously arrested Lamy-Evette and Cottet confessed at Commissioner Lecomte's house. "Tricot, Paul Miette, Guillot, Letort, Constantin, Barraud and Colin Brechedan was there for sure on Wednesday the 12th," Cottet said. "Baillon, Grand C, Francisque, Fortin, the Spaniard, some guy from Genoa, Borge, his wife, Young Fort, Marian, Pastre and Beriquin joined on the 15th," Lamy Evette added. Hoping to get a pardon, Cottet also implicated a number of men who haunted a cafe at Rohan Street. The following day, Lecomte took the confessions to the Committee of Surveillance at the National Convention.

After forty-five consecutive hours of testimony, the Revolutionary Tribunal condemned Douligny and Chambon to the death penalty for "conspiracy to trouble the state." Upon receiving their sentence, the two men denounced Badarel and Francisque, whose real name was Depeyron. Soldiers dragged Badarel from his prison cell at the Conciergerie and delivered him to the Tribunal for questioning. Pressed by Douligny and Chambon, Badarel confessed to hiding jewels in the Widow's Alley. A search near Widow Brule's house uncovered more than one hundred gems.

To reward Douligny and Chambon for the evidence they provided, the Tribunal temporarily stayed their execution. While the police searched for other criminals still at large, the courts condemned Louis Lyre, a twenty-eight-year-old merchant, of receiving stolen property taken from the *Garde-Meuble*. On October 13th, moments before his execution, Lyre implicated Lyon Rouef, his wife, Leyde, Benedict Solomon, Dacosta, Basile, Fontaine, Angeles, senior and junior, and Israel, father and son, of complicity in the sale of the stolen property. Although all received jail sentences, the Tribunal condemned none to death.

On October 16th, the Tribunal judged Francisque, a twenty-seven-year-old marine officer and nephew to the Bishop of Nice, and twenty-two-year-old Badarel, a shoemaker. The court accused Francisque of stealing the Sancy and the Regent Diamonds. Douligny, already condemned to death, swore under oath Francisque had the Regent in his possession. Alexander the Little Cardinal and Gallois confirmed Douligny's story. The President of the Tribunal urged Francisque to confess and reveal the whereabouts of the Regent and the Sancy, but Francisque continued to maintain his innocence.

The Tribunal turned next to Badarel, who broke down under a barrage of questions. He admitted his part in the crime and implicated Francisque.

"There were twenty-eight or thirty of us that night," spoke Badarel in a slow monotone, "and Francisque led the way up the lamp post. I held a candle while Francisque broke open a vitrine with a pair of tongs. He filled his pockets with all he found."

Even in the face of overwhelming evidence, Francisque continued to deny his guilt, accusing Badarel of perjury. Judge Maire urged Francisque to confess and earn the clemency of the court, but Francisque perservered in his innocence.

After a brief deliberation, the Tribunal condemned Depeyron, called Francisque, and Badarel to death. Following a plea for clemency made by the lawyer Gobert, the National Convention on October 18th gave Badarel a reprieve.

On the decided day, guards led Francisque to Place of the Revolution for execution.

"Depeyron, called Francisque, you have been convicted of crimes against the state and have been sentenced to the guillotine. Have you any last words?" the executioner asked.

"I have," answered Francisque. "Let me speak with the authorities? I have valuable information."

Francisque agreed to divulge the hiding place of a sum of gems in exchange for clemency. The President, the Judge and several policemen accompanied the criminal to a house on Saint-Opporteine. Francisque walked up seven flights, entered a public toilet, passed his body through an open window leading to the roof and gathered up two packages of diamonds, which he handed to the President.

On October 23rd, the trial continued. The court convicted a twenty-nine-year-old valet named Joseph Picard and his mistress. On October 30th, Pierre Gallois, alias Matelot, Alexander the Little Cardinal and Francois Mauger began their trial. Under pressure from the authorities, Gallois accused his co-defendants of stealing the Regent and the Sancy.

The night before his sentencing, Gallois tried to kill himself by swallowing a dose of poison smuggled into his cell. The attempt failed.

The next morning in a closing speech, the Public Prosecutor assailed Gallois and Mauger for corrupting the fourteen-year-old Alexander. The Judge condemned both men to death, but mercifully acquitted Alexander, remanding him to a house of correction until his twentieth birthday.

On November 1st, the court convicted Thomas Laurent Meyran, called Grand C, on Douligny's testimony, sentencing him to death. Two days later, as Meyran rose to the scaffold, he saluted in three directions before bravely meeting his fate.

On November 7th, Claude-Melchior Cottet, known as the Little Hunter, found himself in court. Cottet was surprised to be brought to trial since he had co-operated with the authorities. However, the jurors distrusted Cottet. A search of his home revealed a cache of stolen objects that he had failed to hand over to the Committee. In addition, Cottet implicated himself in the theft at the Tuileries the previous August.

A soldier named Brack testified against Cottet. "He tried to bribe me with a gold watch to help him escape before the trial. That Cottet would turn on his mother for a sou."

Based upon additional testimony by Picard and Meyran as well as his own confession, the jury condemned Cottet to the guillotine.

When Cottet begged for a reprieve, the President replied: "Desperate young man, you demand to prolong your guilty days. Prepare yourself for a good end! March to your death with courage."

The next day, at 5:30 in the evening, Cottet demanded to see the President to reassert his innocence in the presence of a priest. He supplied the names of several men fencing the stolen gems. The President refused to grant a pardon. After forcing Cottet to walk past the *Garde-Meuble,* armed soldiers conducted him to the Place of the Revolution for execution.

The last trial took place on November 20th. Paul Miette, the original planner of the burglary, first learned of the arrest of Chambon and Douligny on the 21st of September. After disposing of his share of the loot, Miette went into hiding.

On October 3rd, based on Douligny's testimony, the police ordered Miette's arrest. An informant instructed the authorities to go to a red house on Belleville. Although the house appeared empty, the police broke a window to search inside the building. Hearing loud voices and the shattering of glass, Miette surrendered without a struggle.

Miette denied any wrongdoing, but had difficulty explaining 3,000,000 livres found at his home.

"I have had great luck at gambling," Miette lied to the police.

"He's a thief," blurted out another of the criminals hoping for clemency. "You know the banker on Saint-Honore whose house was robbed. Paul nipped more than 98,000 livres from that caper. He's a bad one, that Miette."

After a brief debate, the Tribunal unanimously condemned Paul Miette to death.

Thus, of the fifty who took part in the theft of the *Garde-Meuble*, seventeen reached trial. The authorities condemned twelve to death. Five received minor sentences. Most of the others escaped.

During September, October and November of 1792, the courts responded to the emotional outcry of the revolutionaries by doling out immediate retribution to all involved in the theft of the *Garde-Meuble*. However, by the middle of 1793, the theft became old news. The courts recognized the thieves strictly had a mercenary motivation. The public demand for capital punishment waned. Thus, Douligny, Chambon, Badarel, Depeyron, Gallois, Mauger and Miette successfully appealed their convictions before the Supreme Court at Beauvais. Due to legal technicalities, all received jail sentences of five years or less. Unfortunately, Louis Lyre, Picard, Picard's mistress, Cottet, and Meyran already had met the guillotine.

Although the trials satisfied the country's need for vengeance, the search for the stolen objects continued. The jewelers Bapst, Minier, and Devoix inventoried the jewels recovered from Depeyron and Badarel. Devoix and the goldsmith Masson tabulated the remaining gems from the *Garde-Meuble*. Only eighty-one stones weighing less than ninety-two carats survived the theft. One forgotten vitrine held several colored stones and pearls and a thirty-two carat sapphire of inferior quality. The thieves had stolen everything else.

On December 10th, 1793, Voulland advised the National Assembly of the recovery of the Regent Diamond by the police the previous day from the home of Bernard Salles.

The thieves had concealed the diamond in an attic window frame in a hole measuring one and one-half thumbs in diameter. Voulland explained an unnamed informant advised the authorities of the hiding place. Unfortunately, the papers of the Revolutionary Committee containing the names of the guilty parties "mysteriously disappeared."[18]

Two members of the Committee carried the Regent Diamond to the National Treasury in an envelope signed with the names of Lelieyre, the mistress to Bernard Salles, Moree, the sister of

Salles and Voilland as well as their own signatures. The Committee deposited the Regent in a box secured with three separate locks for safekeeping. Armed guards at the National Treasury insured the Regent against another theft.

The police remanded Moree and Lelieyre to Saint-Pelagee Prison, where they would remain for almost two years.

Several months after the Regent's recovery, the Committee discovered the Sancy at the home of a man named Tavenal, also called the Turk. The authorities found a number of gems at the home of the Turk's sister, the Widow Leblanc, including a famous diamond from the House of Guise purchased by Colbert from Marie of Lorraine. Tavenal previously had served a term with Paul Miette at LaForce. Apparently, he had taken part in the theft as well. However, the facts concerning the Turk's conviction appear sketchy. Although the records of Tavenal's trial and conviction disappeared, the courts jailed the Turk for a theft against a banker from Lyon a few years later.

In 1795, the Tribunal tried Tavenal's sister along with twenty-six others for complicity in the theft of the Garde-Meuble. The courts freed nine for lack of evidence without a trial. The Jury of Accusation from the Central Tribunal of Paris sentenced Moree, Jeanne Lelievre and Marie-Louise Lelievre as receivers of the Regent. The court also convicted Deschamps or Delcampo, Moyse and Abraham Nunes Dacosta, Guillaume Robert and Horace Moulin, the head of a band of thieves from Marseilles.

At his trial, Guillaume Robert testified a thief named Young Guillot had stolen the Golden Fleece, a magnificent piece of jewelry valued at 3,394,000 livres in the 1791 inventory. The Fleece contained the Great Blue, the rare and unique diamond Louis XIV purchased from Jean Baptiste Tavernier, and a ruby dragon carved by Jacques Buay called the Cote-de-Bretagne, the Coast of Britain. Guillot apparently took the Golden Fleece abroad to be broken up and sold in pieces.[19]

In 1796, a painter named Brard traveling to Germany reported seeing a ruby dragon supposedly taken from the Garde-Meuble. "When I saw the dragon, I became suspicious at once. That man Lancry who showed it to me could not have obtained it by honest means." Lancry, the man with the ruby, happened to be a confederate of Guillot, sent to Hamburg to negotiate the sale of the *Cote-de-Bretagne*. Based on Brard's information, the French government ordered a Minister Reinhardt to arrest Lancry and confiscate the dragon. Reinhardt turned the ruby over to a royalist General, Danican, who later presented the *Cote-de-Bretagne* to Louis XVI's brother, the Count of Provence.

France recovered the greater part of the jewels stolen from the *Garde-Meuble* during September of 1792. The Regent, the Sancy and the *Cote-de-Bretagne* returned to play future historical roles. Some gems such as the Great Blue would be recut and sold abroad. Others such as the Mirror of Portugal disappeared forever. Several of the guilty parties escaped detection and prosecution, and numerous details of the theft remain hazy to this day.[20]

SEVEN

FOLLOWING MARIE ANTOINETTE'S execution, a wave of anarchy swept through France. The period known as the Reign of Terror intensified. While the radical Jacobins crushed the rival Girondins, Danton and Marat's political successor, Maximilien Robespierre, grew in strength. Robespierre, "the Incorruptible One," stood alone, scorning money, hating women—for Robespierre loved only Robespierre. He viciously destroyed his adversaries. On March 24, 1794, his enemy Hebert, a man who made a career of extremism, died at the guillotine. A week later, Camille Desmoulins and Georges-Jacques Danton met their doom. When arrested, Danton prophesied: "Robespierre, the scaffold will claim you."

Robespierre uncovered traitors everywhere. He ordered thousands executed until the country sickened from the stench of death. On July 27th, 1794, the Convention denounced Robespierre with screams of "Down with the tyrant!" Paul Barras, the Commander of the National Guard, arrested Robespierre, who met his death at the guillotine within the week.

After ending Robespierre's Reign of Terror, Barras became an instant hero. The Council named him as a member of the Directory, the executive arm of the new government.

When Louis XVI's younger brother, the Count of Provence, calling himself Louis XVIII, vowed to return from exile in Verona, royalist sympathizers in the city of Toulon revolted. Barras sent his protégé, General Napoleon Bonaparte, to silence the royalist opposition with his artillery. Bonaparte's victory on October 5th, 1795, gained Bonaparte immediate recognition. At Barras's instigation, the Convention promoted the young general to commander of the French army in Italy.

At one of his parties, Barras had introduced the General to his former mistress, Josephine de Beauharnais, a charming Creole widow from Martinique, six years Napoleon's senior. following a whirlwind romance, Napoleon married Josephine in a civil ceremony before departing to the Italian front.

During this period, France battled England and Austria on numerous fronts. In fact, the country maintained fourteen separate armies on the field. The costs of the war proved enormous. Although the National Convention had confiscated money and property from the emigré aristocrats, the army's needs strained the national budget. To keep the army afloat, the Directory elected to use the diamonds in the Public Treasury for funding loans. An inventory taken in 1795 had valued the Regent at 6,000,000 francs and the remaining diamonds in the Treasury at 10,000,000 francs.

Under a complex financial arrangement, the Directory authorized Adjutant-General Parceval to negotiate a series of loans using the diamonds as collateral. Parceval deposited the fifty-five-carat pear-shaped Sancy Diamond with the Marquess of Iranda in Madrid as security for 1,000,000 francs. Parceval deposited the Regent in a bank at Bale for remittance to a German liquor dealer named Treskow in exchange for 4,000,000 francs. Treskow demanded additional security, forcing Parceval to deposit additional stones to complete the loan.[21]

In 1796, the Directory sent Parceval to Berlin to redeem the Regent after obtaining funds through the firm of Carrier, Bezard and Company. In 1797, the Treasury again ran dry, and the Regent collateralized a loan with a Dutchman named Valenberghem to purchase cavalry horses. Supposedly Valenberghem displayed the Regent in a glass case at his house for his friends in Amsterdam to admire. After returning the diamond to France in 1800, an acquaintance questioned how Valenberghem dared risk the Regent to theft. The financier explained the stone in the case had been a glass facsimile. The real Regent remained hidden on his wife, suspended around her neck beneath her blouse.[22]

Until Barras befriended him, few recognized the full measure of the tiny Corsican named Napoleon Bonaparte. Born August 15, 1769, and educated in mathematics at a French military school, Napoleon hungered for adventure. He possessed the ability to subordinate the detail demanded of a military engineer to an overriding sense of destiny. "I am conscious of no limit to the work I can get through," he wrote in his memoirs. His magnetism dominated those around him. "I am afraid of him," confessed Augereau, one of his chief lieutenants. "I don't understand his ascendancy over me, so that I feel struck down just by the flash of his eye." General Junot wrote: "He is the sort of man of whom nature is sparing, who only appears on earth in intervals of centuries."

During the Italian campaign, his poorly trained and inadequately provisioned ragtag assortment of 37,000 men crossed the Alps and annihilated the surprised enemy. Napoleon utilized simple offensive techniques—rapid troop concentration, immediate attack and division of the enemy forces.

Following the victorious Italian campaign and a less successful Egyptian war, this rising political star returned to France. Crowds greeted him as a symbol of conquest wherever he went. The revolution of 1789 had brought little financial improvement to the lower classes in the cities. Only the middle class and the Directors actually prospered. The poor mocked the regal trappings of the corrupt Directors in their gold and velvet costumes, calling them the "Five Majesties." Many of the underclasses believed only the firm hand of a single leader could return France to greatness.

On November 9th, 1799, the Council of Ancients appointed Napoleon Commander of the Paris Garrison. The General promised to uphold the Republic to the cheers of his army. After the ceremony had ended, Napoleon received an emissary from Barras at the doorway of the Tuileries. The man begged safe passage from Paris for the Directors. Napoleon responded: "What have you done with this France which I left you in its full splendor? I left you peace, and I find war; I left you victories, and I find defeats! I left you millions from Italy; I find everywhere spoilation and misery." Mounting his horse, he left the crowd whispering his praises while he returned to his wife.

In a *coup d'etat* engineered by Napoleon's brother Lucien on November 10th, 1799, the National Council ousted the Directory and named Napoleon Bonaparte, Emmanuel-Joseph Sieyes and Roger Ducos as Consuls in their place. The public recognized only Bonaparte.

Sieyes nominated Napoleon as First Consul. On December 12th, Napoleon accepted. Sieyes and Ducos resigned shortly thereafter. When the First Consul established residency in the Tuileries, France merely exchanged one aristocracy for another. Napoleon commented on the Republic: "It's a will-o-the-wisp with which the French have become infatuated, but which will pass away like so many others. They require glory, the satisfaction of their vanity, but about freedom they know nothing."

Victory followed victory for the First Consul. "I am destined to change the face of the earth, at least that is my belief," Napoleon confided to his brother Joseph. On June 14th, 1800, Napoleon's troops crushed France's enemy Austria at Marengo. As his popularity with the masses grew, Napoleon became a danger to both the leftist radicals and the rightest monarchists. Plots against him multiplied. Guards discovered a poisoned snuffbox on his desk. A few months later, the police arrested two groups of radical nationalists for plotting his death. In December, three royalist sympathizers from Brittany directed a wagon full of explosives toward the First Consul's coach as he drove to the opera. The explosion killed twenty-two and wounded fifty-six, although Napoleon and his retinue escaped harm.

By the beginning of 1801, Europe had begun to surrender to the French. At the Peace of Luneville on February 9th, Austria recognized Belgium and Luxembourg as French territory. A pact with Spain gave Louisiana to France. On March 2nd, 1802, England signed the Treaty of Amiens with France. Soon the rest of France's enemies followed suit. Prussia signed a treaty on

May 23rd, Bavaria the next day, Turkey on October 9th and
Russia on October 11th. The war had ended.

The people of Paris welcomed their thirty-two-year-old con-
queror with cheers of *"Vive Napoleon!"* Bonaparte had delivered
the glory he had promised France.

Choosing 400,000 francs worth of diamonds recently returned
from Holland, Napoleon presented them as gifts for the pleni-
potentiaries who had signed the peace treaties. The First Consul selected the Regent for himself. He ordered Lieutenant-
Colonel Edgar Nitot to design a consular sword. The hilt of the
sword held the Regent along with two perfectly matched sixteen-
and-a-half-carat brilliants and seven other major diamonds.
The total diamond weight of the sword exceeded two hundred
fifty-four carats. The artist Baron Antoine Jean Gros painted a
portrait of the First Consul dressed in a golden-brocaded red
coat and white pants with the consular sword strapped to his left
hip. Today, that painting hangs in the Museum of the Legion of
Honor in Paris.

Peace proved short-lived for Napoleon. When the English
supported royalist sympathizers in France, Napoleon executed
an innocent Bourbon prince in reprisal. From his exile, Louis
XVIII cried out for England and Austria to punish Napoleon as
a criminal and a usurper. For years, Josephine, still an aristocrat
at heart, urged Napoleon to declare himself emperor. Brooding
about the continuing conspiracies of the royalists, the First
Consul determined to heed his wife and provide continuity to
his reign.

On November 30th, 1804, Pope Pius VII formally married
Napoleon and Josephine under the laws of Catholicism, sanctify-
ing the civil ceremony performed years earlier. On December
2nd, dressed in white silk embroidered robes and sparkling with
the state jewelry once worn by the Bourbons, Josephine accompanied Napoleon along the cold and foggy streets to Notre
Dame in a crystal and gold carriage for the coronation ceremony.[23]

The jeweler Marguerite created the Empress's crown while
Leroy and Raimbaud produced her emerald parures. Fuming
with jealousy, Napoleon's sisters reluctantly lifted Josephine's

train, but only after their brother assigned ladies-in-waiting to carry theirs too. Nitot, Marguerite and Biennais supplied the Emperor's crown regalia. Napoleon, dressed in a purple robe lined with ermine and a plumed diamond-studded hat, vowed to govern "in accordance with the interests, happiness, and the glory of the French people."

After receiving the Pope's blessing, Napoleon took the crown from the Pope's hands and placed it on his own head, declaring himself Emperor of France.

"Ah Joseph!" said the Emperor to his brother following the coronation ceremony. "If only our father were to see us."

From a childhood of poverty, the thirty-five-year-old Napoleon had become emperor of the most powerful country in Europe. Such exultation passed quickly. England and Austria again declared war on France. The English navy under Admiral Nelson annihilated the French fleet at Trafalgar in October of 1805. Napoleon's troops recovered with an overwhelming victory at Austerlitz. Although the French navy was no match for the English, the French army appeared invincible on land. Napoleon crushed the Prussians at Jena and Auerstedt.

Napoleon rewarded his marshals and family with the spoils of war. He appointed his brother Joseph King of Naples and his brother Louis King of Holland. Other family members received the Dukedoms of Wurttemberg, Piombino and Bavaria.

On December 19th, 1806, Napoleon triumphantly entered Warsaw. In Poland, the Emperor bedded Marie Waliuska, who later gave birth to his bastard child. After signing a peace treaty with Russia, Napoleon concentrated his war efforts on Spain, forcing King Ferdinand VII to abdicate. In 1808, the Emperor placed Joseph on the throne of Spain and named his brother-in-law Murat as King of Naples in Joseph's place.

For some time, Napoleon had dreamed of providing an heir to the French throne. Marie Waliuska's bastard son testified to his virility. Although Josephine had two children by her previous marriage, the aftermath of an illness prevented Josephine from another pregnancy. Intrigues against his life and an overwhelming urge for the continuity of rule convinced Napo-

leon the country required an heir. Although he loved Josephine,
he loved France more.

"Josephine, you know we must separate. France demands it of
me. I shall always love you," the Emperor coaxed.

"I'd rip out the eyes of any woman who shares your bed,"
countered Josephine.

In December of 1809, Josephine reluctantly granted Napoleon a divorce. The Emperor considered seeking the hand of
Anna, the fifteen-year-old sister of Tsar Alexander I of Russia,
but his final choice fell to Marie-Louise, the eighteen-year-old
daughter of Emperor Francis I of Austria. Friends warned Napoleon that Marie-Louise had been brought up to hate him, but he
refused to be dissuaded. Although plain in appearance, Marie-
Louise had striking blue eyes, a pretty complexion and a mild
temper. She consented to wed her much older husband, a man
she had never seen.

On March 11, 1810, Marie-Louise married the absent Napoleon, represented at the ceremony by one of his marshals in
Vienna. A few days later, the Empress began the fifteen-day
journey to Paris, accompanied by eighty-three coaches, for a
second wedding ceremony.

Prior to the wedding, Napoleon requested Daru, the minister
of his household, to inventory all available jewels. Napoleon
purchased an additional 6,600,000 francs of jewels to ornament
his bride for the civil ceremony held at St. Cloud on April 1st.

On June 15th, 1811, the court jewelers dismounted Napoleon's
consular sword. The Emperor ordered the jewelers to put the
Regent in a new sword hung from a baldric of white velvet
covered with rose diamonds. Napoleon fastidiously designed
regulations to insure the safety of the sword and the other
Crown Jewels.

Less than one year after the wedding, one hundred and one
cannon shots roared through Paris announcing the birth of the
son Josephine had failed to provide. Napoleon showered his
wife with gifts, including a magnificent 275-carat diamond
necklace.[24]

Napoleon appeared to be at the zenith of power. He possessed a charming young wife and the heir he always wanted. The French Empire extended from the North Sea to the Bay of Naples and eastward to the Adriatic. He was King of Italy and Protector of the Confederation of the Rhine. Austria and Prussia paid tribute to him. His brothers ruled Spain, Westphalia and Holland.

Despite this apparent strength, Napoleon's victories had stretched the Empire to the breaking point. The battles of Jena and Austerlitz had thinned the ranks of his veterans, sapping the vitality of the Grand Army. Even the Emperor's wonderful vitality had begun to weaken.

Like vultures plucking at the heart of Prometheus, Napoleon's enemies united against the weakened giant. First, Austria attacked at Wagram, but Napoleon proved victorious.

"They have agreed to meet at my grave, but as yet they dare not gather there," Napoleon mocked.

Always eager to assume the offensive, Napoleon invaded Russia in 1812. At first, victory came easily. The Russians retreated against the relentless French advance. By the time the French army reached Moscow, her supplies had been depleted. Napoleon planned to resupply his army in Moscow. However, the Emperor underestimated the resolve of Tsar Alexander. Adopting a scorched-earth policy, the Russians burned Moscow, forcing the French to retreat through the heart of winter.

The first snows fell on November 5th. When the cold killed the horses, the cavalry marched on foot. Thousands of starving French troops died during the freezing Russian winter. Cossack guerrillas shot any surviving stragglers. On December 5th, Napoleon relinquished command of the army to his brother-in-law Murat. He departed by sleigh for home to hold off the threat of a potential revolution in Paris. In his pocket he carried a vial of poison, vowing to kill himself rather than be taken alive by his enemies.

Russia had decimated the French army. When Prince Metternich of Austria urged Napoleon to sue for peace, the Emperor testily replied: "You do not know what goes on in the mind of a soldier. A man such as I does not take much heed of the lives of a

million men." Thus rebuked, 600,000 Prussian, Russian, Austrian
and English troops massed to invade France.

Watching his empire collapse like a deck of carefully balanced cards on a windy day, Napoleon struggled to maintain
the equilibrium. His once powerful body battled the ravages of
premature old age. His torso thickened, and his mind slowed. "I
do not fear to acknowledge that I have made war too long. I had
conceived vast projects; I wished to secure to France the empire
of the world. I was mistaken. Those projects were not propor-
tioned to the numerical force of our population," he wrote.

Napoleon retired to Fontainebleau to plan a strategy for his
diminished army of 50,000 to hold off the enemy forces. Marshal
Ney begged the Emperor to abdicate and save France. At first,
Napoleon refused to listen to his officers. After recognizing the
hopelessness of his cause, he drank a vial of poison but survived.

While the Emperor struggled to accept defeat, Empress Marie-
Louise escaped Paris in the state coach on March 28th of 1814.
Accompanied by her children, two chamberlains, several ladies
of the court and an armed contingent of 1,000 cavalrymen, the
Empress made for Rambouillet, followed by twelve baggage
trains and the coronation coach stuffed with her wardrobe,
household items, personal jewelry, gold from the Public Treasury and the state jewelry. Napoleon's sword containing the
Regent Diamond sat beside her in the coach.

When the Empress reached the city of Chartres, a distance of
fifty miles from Paris, Napoleon's brothers Jerome and Joseph
along with their families joined the party. The coaches containing
this Bonaparte contingent next hurried along the mud-soaked
roads to reach the city of Blois, where on April 2nd, Napoleon's
mother, Letizia, and his brother Louis joined the exodus. In a
near state of panic, Louis begged the family to flee to an Austrian
fortress without delay.

On April 9th, Marie-Louise expressed her concern to Napoleon's aide Meneval about the safety of the treasure in her
charge. During the past week, her husband, the Emperor, had
abdicated the throne. Marauding Cossacks and thieves roamed
the unprotected roads searching for booty. Although Caulaincourt

had formed a provisional government, France simmered with unrest. The gold and jewels in her wagon train would make a fine prize.

Napoleon's sword containing the Regent Diamond represented the richest treasure of all. The Regent had crowned kings and adorned queens. The sword itself signified Napoleon's power and strength.

Marie-Louise recognized the sword's prominence in French history. Unfortunately, the length of the blade made the sword difficult to conceal. The Empress ordered Meneval to separate the jeweled hilt from the steel blade. "Sir, you must perform the surgery." Because Meneval lacked the proper tools, he snapped the hilt off the blade, using the andirons from the Empress's apartment fireplace.

In his book *Napoleon and Marie-Louise* published in 1843, Meneval wrote that he concealed the hilt, valued at more than 2,000,000 francs, beneath his coat. Likewise, Marie-Louise wore several valuable stones beneath her outfit. "They would not dare to search my person," she explained to Meneval.

The journey from Blois to Orleans proved treacherous. At the town of Beaugency, the Cossacks isolated one of the royal carriages.

"Halt!" ordered a bearded Russian dressed in a long fur coat. His right hand brandished a sword. Three armed Cossacks rode at his side.

"Whoa," the French driver coaxed his team of horses to stop. "I want no trouble. Take what you want and let me be."

The Cossacks rifled through the carriage but found little of value. They took a few inexpensive trinkets.

"Where's the gold?" snarled the Russian in broken French.

"There's just dresses and the like," explained the driver. "For all I know, the gold's in Orleans by now."

"Damn!" The Russian swore at the driver. "Let's go." The four men rode away in the opposite direction.

On April 11th, while Marie-Louise rested at Orleans, the provisional government advised Napoleon at Fountainebleau of his exile to Elba.

"You must write Meneval to return the state jewels via our emissary," one of the officials demanded. The Emperor reluctantly agreed.

When Meneval informed Marie-Louise of the Emperor's orders, she separated her personal jewelry from the state jewelry.

On Easter Sunday, an official of the provisional government named Dudon confiscated the Empress's wagons, which contained 13,400,000 francs of gold, silver holloware, snuff boxes, diamond rings and imperial jewels, including the Regent. Dudon then presented himself to the Empress's lady-in-waiting demanding the pearl necklace worn by Marie-Louise. The necklace, which cost nearly 500,000 francs, had been given to the Empress by Napoleon shortly after the birth of her son. When the lady-in-waiting delivered the message, Marie-Louise took off the necklace, saying: "Hand it to him and say nothing."

After Dudon's departure, as the Empress prepared to depart for Rambouillet, Napoleon's treasurer, Guillaume Peyrusse, arrived at her apartment in Orleans to retrieve the Emperor's personal fortune. When Marie-Louise greeted him, the hint of a tear formed in the corner of her eye.

"Don't worry," she said. "I won't cry. It would embarrass both of us, but an Empress has feelings just like everyone else. I know I shall never see the Emperor again. Had he been a lesser man, one without so expansive a view of the world, we might still be together." The Empress paused and smiled. "Yet, I wonder if I would have admired him as much."

The Empress explained Dudon already had taken everything of value except for 6,000,000 francs in currency that had been her personal property.[25]

Since the Treasurer traveled without the benefit of a military escort, the Empress suggested the safest action would be for her to take the currency to Austria and return one-half at a later date. "I shall need funds to cover my expenses," Marie-Louise explained.

"I see your point, Madame," the Treasurer said. "To carry so much money would only benefit the Cossacks who ravage the highways."

While soldiers escorted Napoleon to exile in Elba and Marie-Louise to Austria, Louis XVIII's younger brother, the Count of Artois, entered Paris to cheering crowds. Madame Chateaubriand aptly remarked: "The moment it was certain that the lion was chained, sufficient words could not be found to damn him for whom incense had been so lately been burned." The Senate ousted Napoleon, declaring a constitutional monarchy under Louis XVIII.

On April 12th, the Count of Artois entered the Tuileries. When asked if the long day's activities had tired him, he replied: "Why should I be tired? It is the first happy day I have had in thirty years."

Artois immediately imposed decrees restoring emigré property. Louis XVIII entered Paris on May 2nd, 1814, after promising to uphold the constitution. The sixty-year-old gout-ridden King sought to heal France's wounds with a regime of moderation. Unfortunately, Louis lacked the power to check the excesses of the royalists who had plundered the homes of the Bonapartists. Leftists and revolutionaries became increasingly dissatisfied with his rule.

Napoleon chafed from the boredom of exile at Elba. He hated inactivity. His ambition cried out for fulfillment. His first wife, Josephine, had died. His second, Marie-Louise, tired of waiting and eventually chose Count Neipperg to be her lover. Marie-Louise's infidelity rankled the Emperor. Napoleon later would confess to Metternich: "Everything confirms that I have made an irreparable mistake in marrying an archduchess of Austria. I wished to unite the past and present, Gothic prejudice and the institutions of our century. I see now the full extent of my error."

Spies advised Napoleon the Grand Army would welcome his return. The middle class yearned for the past splendor of the Empire. While Louis XVIII reclaimed several estates confiscated during the revolution, Napoleon seized an opportunity to escape. Security on Elba proved weak. Accompanied by seven ships and 1,100 men, Napoleon landed on the coast of France near Cannes on March 1, 1815.

"There is no precedent in history for what I am about to do,"
Napoleon told his secretary. "I can count on public astonishment,
the state of public opinion, the resentment against the allies, the
affection of my soldiers, and the attachment to the Empire
which lingers everywhere in France. . . . I shall arrive in Paris
without firing a shot."

At Grenoble, Napoleon greeted an army sent to capture him
with the words: "Soldiers of the Fifth, I am your Emperor. Do
you recognize me? If there is among you a soldier who would
like to kill his Emperor, here I am." The battalion lowered its
arms and shouted: *"Vive l'Empereur!"*

In six days, Napoleon had marched more than two hundred
miles. When Louis XVIII sent Marshal Ney to arrest Napoleon,
Ney boasted: "I shall bring Napoleon to Paris in an iron cage."
However, when the two met in person, Ney succumbed to
Napoleon's strength of will, proclaiming: "The Bourbon cause
is lost forever."

Louis XVIII recognized the impossibility of stopping Napoleon's advance without a full civil war. On March 19th, after
receiving word Napoleon had reached Fontainebleau, Louis
departed the Tuileries for Ghent, taking the Regent Diamond
and other jewels with him. As two noblemen half-carried the fat
old King to his carriage, Louis promised his few remaining
supporters: "I shall see you again before long."

The European powers banded against the outlaw Corsican.
By dint of his indominable personality and military skills,
Napoleon held off the combined Russian, Prussian, English and
Austrian forces for several months. Ailing from piles and syscitus,
an inflamation of the bladder and urinary tract, the Emperor
fought to maintain his throne, but costly victories decimated
his army.

On Sunday, June 18th, General Blucher and the Duke of
Wellington's forces cornered the French army at Waterloo. Napoleon suffered a terrible defeat. He wept for his fallen comrades
and mourned the fact that he had survived. Abdicating his
throne a second time, he thought of escaping to America, but
procrastinated. When his enemies came to arrest him, Napoleon

escaped to Rochefort, where he surrendered to Captain Maitland of the British man-of-war *Bellerophon.*

Napoleon wrote the Prince Regent of England seeking sanctuary:

> Pursued by the factions which divide my country and by the hostility of the powers of Europe, I have finished my political career. I come like Themistocles to sit at the hearth of the British people. I put myself under the protection of the laws which I claim from your Royal Highness as the most powerful, constant and generous of my enemies."

The British refused Napoleon's request. On August 4th, 1815, Captain Maitland transferred Napoleon to the *Northumberland.* On August 8th, Napoleon departed for his final exile in St. Helena, a tiny, isolated volcanic island in the South Atlantic.

Napoleon detested St. Helena. Within a few years, he became an old man. "The oil in my lamp has run dry," he dictated to his secretary. Ailments attacked him on a dozen fronts. Toothaches, skin eruptions, headaches, vomiting, dysentery, cold extremities, an ulcer and cancer followed with increasing severity. He became morose and irritable. During his final months, he vomited constantly.

On May 21, 1821, at the age of fifty-two, Napoleon's suffering ended. An autopsy revealed cancer of the stomach and intestine. One ulcer had cut a hole almost one-quarter of an inch wide through the lining of his stomach. His bladder was small and contained several stones.

It seemed appropriate for Napoleon, a man who ruled by "absolute unity of power, constant supervision and fear," to have worn the Regent in the hilt of his sword. Like Alexander the Great before him, Napoleon possessed one of the greatest military minds of all time.

EIGHT

A LIFE OF WANDERING had wearied Louis XVIII. Born Louis Stanislas Xavier on November 17, 1755, the then Count of Provence fled Paris after the revolution of 1789 and his brother Louis XVI's subsequent arrest. Shuffled from country to country, Louis XVIII lost his youth struggling to regain the French crown. Forced to seek refuge in Westphalia, Courland, Poland, Sweden, Austria and England, a sick and disillusioned Louis returned to France to reclaim his throne.

At 9:00 in the morning on July 8, 1815, following Napoleon's abdication, soldiers hauled down the tricolor flag above the Tuileries. At 3:30 in the afternoon, a cannon burst announced the arrival of the King's coach. Cheering crowds lined the street. The King's younger brother, the Count of Artois, and the King's nephew, the Duke of Berry, rode beside him.

The journey in the coach proved hot and uncomfortable. Sweat dripped from Louis's forehead down his pudgy cheeks. The acid in his system caused his gout-ridden foot to burn. His body ached.

"You look uncomfortable, brother," remarked the Count of Artois.

Louis nodded in silent agreement. He recalled the years of exile and relived the deaths of friends and family. His past humiliation and loneliness far outweighed the pains of old age. "So long, so long," the King muttered aloud. "I've waited so long."

As one of his first acts, Louis placed the Crown jewels he had carried with him into exile under the stewardship of the jewelers Meniere and Bapst. Louis also ordered the jewelers to remove the letter "N" from Napoleon's snuffboxes and to dismount Marie-Louise's diamond and emerald parures.

An inventory taken in the presence of Baron Hue revealed many pieces from the 1791 inventory either had been stolen during the burglary of the *Garde-Meuble,* pawned by the revolutionary government or given as gifts by Napoleon to his officers and ministers.

From the remaining jewels, Louis selected ten diamonds from one of Napoleon's swords. He requested the jewelers to design a star-shaped medallion, which he presented to the Duke of Wellington in gratitude for the Duke's victory over Napoleon at Waterloo.

Louis asked Evrard and Frederic Bapst to create a coronation crown containing the Regent Diamond. The King later decided to forego a formal ceremony, choosing to concentrate on the country's serious problems. Thus, Louis XVIII made few alterations in the remaining jewels, which were returned to the public treasury for safekeeping. Because his wife had died in 1810, the King allowed the royal princesses to use the Crown Jewels from time to time. Louis XVIII rarely wore jewelry himself.[26]

Louis hoped to soothe the wounds of the past. Unfortunately, age and ill health worked against him. He had waited too long to rule. The ultra-royalists under his brother's leadership emasculated Louis's reign and fomented violent unrest.

On February 13, 1820, a fanatic stabbed the Count of Artois's son, Charles Ferdinand, the Duke of Berry, who died the next day. Following the assassination, the Count grew increasingly militant, seizing an even greater share of power for the ultra-royalist cause.

As gout, vericose veins and obesity racked Louis XVIII's body with pain, he survived until September 16, 1824, by dint of will. The moment the old King died, an usher opened the door to Louis's bedroom and announced the entry of the Count of

Artois with the words: "Gentlemen, the King." The sixty-seven-year-old Artois entered the room as King Charles X.

Custom prohibited the King from remaining in the same building with his brother's body. Thus, Charles immediately departed the Tuileries for Saint Cloud. On September 19th, he returned to attend his brother's funeral. Horses were draped in black, buckles darkened and swords bronzed for the solemn ceremony. On September 23rd, a procession carried Louis XVIII's casket to the burial vault at Saint Denis to rest along the side of his brother Louis XVI, his nephew the Duke of Barry and his sister-in-law Marie Antoinette.

Charles X, born October 9th, 1757, as Charles Philippe, had been a strong-willed hedonistic youth. Even as a child, he had an innate sense of cunning.

Court etiquette forbade appearing before the King with a covered head. However, the future Charles X once bet his brothers he could appear before his grandfather King Louis XV wearing a hat. When the boys accepted the dare, Charles appeared before the King in a hat:

"Grandfather, don't you think I look becoming in a hat?" Charles asked. "My brothers argue to the contrary."

"But the hat fits you perfectly," said the King.

"In that case, Sire, will you please have the goodness to tell my brothers, because they will not believe me."

Charles won his bet. The King was the first to laugh at his grandson's ingenuity.

As a youth, Artois lived for pleasure. Although married at the age of sixteen to a princess of Sardinia, the Count carried on a liaison with the Viscountess of Polastron for many years. Rumor also linked his name sexually to his sister-in-law Marie Antoinette. Artois's arrogance led to at least one duel in which he received a minor wound. His drinking and gambling shocked Paris and set the pace for decadent court morality. His irresponsibility contributed heavily to the spirit of revolution that killed his older brother Louis XVI.

After fleeing France in July of 1789, Artois traveled to Belgium and Switzerland before receiving asylum from his father-in-law in Sardinia. He behaved well in Turin, possibly because his father-in-law provided him with an allowance of 30,000 francs per month. Eventually morality bored him, and he left for Coblenz to meet his mistress.

On March 27, 1804, Viscountess Polatron died, and Artois's life changed. He vowed to give himself to God and the quest for the return to a Bourbon crown. The Count of Artois ceased being a playboy to become the leading proponent of the ultra-royalists. His espousal of the emigré cause continued through-out his exile and during his brother's reign.

Following the funeral ceremony of his brother Louis XVIII, Charles X returned to Paris in full military uniform astride an Arabian horse. The sun's rays sparkled from the metalic buttons on his coat. One hundred and one guns announced Charles's arrival. As he surveyed the crowds outside the Tuileries, Charles silently recounted the years of torture suffered by his family. Radicals had murdered both his brother and his son. He vowed to make the revolutionaries pay. Sullenly, he dismounted and waved to his countrymen, dissembling the hate within him. Never again should a French king be subjected to such abuse. Charles promised himself he would regain full regal power. He recognized the clergy required more authority to still the out-bursts of the masses. He would provide the necessary support. Besides, Charles believed religion to be the first need of moral man. Thus, a priest became Minister of Education. Charles determined to re-establish the full political role of the aristocracy. "I would rather hew wood than be a king under the conditions of the King of England," he professed.

Recognizing the importance of outward appearances, Charles planned an elaborate coronation to symbolize the tone of his reign. On May 20, 1825, the King discontinued the session of the Chamber to enable its officers to assist in the ceremony.

An inventory of the Crown Jewels completed by the Chamber peers and the Council of Deputies required thirteen pages and included 68,812 stones weighing 18,750 carats valued at 20,900,260 francs. Charles selected the magnificent crown Evrard and Frederic Bapst had created for his brother Louis XVIII for the coronation. The Regent Diamond glistened from a *fleur-de-lis* in its center. The sword made for the coronation contained 1,576 brilliant diamonds weighing more than 330 carats. The settings had been so delicately executed the sword felt as smooth as ivory. The jewelry prepared for Charles X's ceremony rivaled that of any monarch in any land throughout the ages.[27]

The coronation began May 28th at Rheims with Charles attending vesper services. City officials presented him with a welcoming gift of pears and champagne. As a special dispensation, the grateful monarch ordered fifty prisoners released from the city's prisons.

The following day, Rheims bustled with excitement. At 6:00 in the morning, officials opened the cathedral doors. Representatives from every major country marched into the building. Marshal Moncey carried the King's sword. Soult carried the royal sceptre, the Hand of Justice and the crown.

The five-hour ceremony began at 7:00 A.M. Archbishop Latil blessed the diamond-studded sword, strapping it to the King's waist. The monarch kissed the weapon and placed it on the altar. Next, the Archbishop annointed the King's head with oil, making the sign of the cross on his breast, back, shoulders and arms. Finally, the priest crowned the King to cries of "May the King live forever." Servants released a thousand doves in the cathedral. Trumpets blared, and guns roared to announce the coronation of King Charles X.

Charles loved horses and the hunt. He enjoyed whist and billiards. Looking every inch an aristocrat, dignified and handsome, he lacked ability. The years in exile had clouded his thinking.

By 1830, plots rose against Charles. He faced opposition with the stubborness of his Bourbon ancestry. On March 1, he complained to the Chamber: "Do you not know how malevolence interprets my actions and even my words; that everywhere, and above all in Paris, intrigues are being formed against my authority. Oh, I swear to you, I cannot endure it. It is enough to make one give it all up and leave."

When the King's granddaughter heard about the speech, she

jokingly put a sign in her window, "House to let." How close to the truth she would be.

At 1:00 in the afternoon on March 2nd, the King convened the Chamber at the Louvre. Although his shrill voice lacked resonance and he read clumsily, his strong words shocked the audience: "I shall brook no opposition in these matters," Charles announced. He called for an increase in taxation, suspension of the freedom of the press, and a return to absolute monarchy. During the speech, his diamond studded hat fell to the floor near the Duke of Orleans, who picked it up and held it until the speech ended. The more liberal members of the audience greeted the King's proposals with cold silence. Others urged Charles to reconsider his stance.

On July 25th, Charles X signed into law the measures outlined in his March speech. The new ordinances struck Paris like a bombshell, exploding into public outrage. Crowds gathered in front of the Foreign Ministry, chanting: "Long live the Charter! Down with the regime." On July 27th, the *Globe* and the *National* newspapers published without authorization. Unlike the revolution of 1789, skilled trades led the way to the Revolution of 1830.

The King reacted by occupying the major streets with troops. The mobs of Paris countered by seizing Notre Dame and cutting down trees to form barricades around its perimeter.

"It is no longer a riot; it is revolution," warned Marshal Marmont, Charles's commanding general. The King refused to negotiate. While the battle raged in the Paris streets, the King played whist as usual, assuming eventual victory.

In the seaport city of Caen, the tricolor flag of the revolutionaries already had replaced the Bourbon white. The political situation appeared ominous. On July 28th, the King ordered the Crown Jewels to be taken from the Ministry of Finance and delivered by coach to his country residence at Saint Cloud. On Thursday morning the 29th, Marmont pleaded with the King: "The honor of the crown can still be saved. Tomorrow, it will be too late." The King refused to rescind the July proclamation. When the diplomat Tallyrand watched the royal troops retreat on the *Rue de Rivoli*, he commented: "Note that on July 29, 1830, at five minutes past noon, the elder branch of the Bourbons ceased to reign over France."

Pro-Bourbon ministers sped to Saint Cloud to urge the King to grant immediate concessions. Charles again refused.

On July 30th, the Chamber of Deputies deposed Charles X and began debate on a successor. On August 5th, a militia of 60,000 under the leadership of General Pajol arrived outside Charles's quarters brandishing pikes and halberds demanding retribution. Charles wisely abdicated, agreeing to leave France forever. Commissioners negotiated with General Pajol for the return of the jewels in exchange for the royal family's safe passage.

The King took leave of his loyal supporters and departed by ship for England. On October 25th, he and his family left England for the Hradschin Palace near Prague. His final days there proved to be long and dull. On November 6, 1836, the seventy-nine-year-old King died of complications from Asiatic cholera. Doctors removed his heart, placing it in a small box. His body was embalmed and buried in a lead coffin in a Franciscan monastery outside the city of Goritz.

Even as Charles made his way to England, General Pajol and the triumphant mob returned to Paris, depositing the Crown Jewels in the Central Treasury of the Finance Ministry. Officials locked the Regent Diamond in a strongbox requiring five separate keys as a security measure. The jeweler Evrard Bapst held two keys, a government executive named Lazard kept two, and M. Kessner retained the final key.

After much discussion, the Chamber named Louis Philippe, the Duke of Orleans, as Lieutenant-General of the Realm. Louis Philippe walked rather than rode to the *Hotel de Ville* for his installation ceremony. Lafayette, the hero of the revolution of 1789, wrapped a tri-color scarf around the Lieutenant-General's neck, embracing him to the cheers of the crowds. On August 7th, 1830, the Chamber proclaimed the Lieutenant-General as King Louis Philippe I, "King of the French by the grace of God and the will of the people." After Louis Philippe signed a new charter, four marshals of the realm approached him bearing the royal sceptre, the crown of Charles X containing the Regent

Diamond, the royal sword and the Hand of Justice, symbols of the beginning of his reign.

King Louis Philippe cared little for the trappings of authority. He opened the royal palace for any to visit. He replaced the formal *fleur-de-lis* decorations on the walls with more mundane strawberry leaves. He ordered the royal lillies erased from the side of his carriage. Neither he nor his wife wore the Crown Jewels, which apparently had been stored on the premises of Bapst and Company at *Quay de l'Ecole*. An armed guard posted at the doorway ensured the safety of the treasure inside the building.

In 1832, under a new law, officials transferred the Crown Jewels inside a strongbox to a vault at the Louvre for safekeeping. At a later date, officials moved the Crown Jewels to the Tuileries along with the royal family's personal belongings. The jewels were hidden inside a locked strongbox buried within a wall safe. The treasurer Verbois, the jeweler Constant Bapst and an inspector named Marechal each held a key to the locks.[28]

Between 1835 and 1846, six separate attempts to assassinate the "Citizen King" failed. The Legitimists on the right espoused the Bourbon cause. The Bonapartists on the left supported Napoleon's nephew Louis Napoleon. Republicans and socialists sought to end the monarchy entirely. When Louis Philippe attempted to reinstate dynastic rule, he alienated liberal French opinion, the heart and soul of his power base.

The political analyst Lamartine summed up the country's dissatisfaction with the explanation: "France is bored." The Austrian diplomat Metternich wrote: "The Orleanist regime rested neither on popular enthusiasm, the authority of the plebiscite, the glory of Napoleon, nor the sanction of a legitimate dynasty. Its durability rests solely upon accident."

The King had been the protector of the middle class. When royal troops fired upon an unarmed crowd of protesters on February 23rd, 1848, the country rose against the King. After a few days of insurrection, Louis Philippe abdicated.

Sensing the potential danger of theft, Louis Philippe's treasurer Verbois shifted the royal family's personal jewels from the

Tuileries to the home of a friend living on the Street of Pyramids. When Verbois returned for the Crown Jewels, he saw crowds of people jamming the streets everywhere.

A mob had broken into the Tuileries to plunder, but it showed more interest in the royal wine supply than the Crown Jewels. The cellar contained almost 10,000 bottles of wine. "There's wine enough for an army," shouted one of the bolder intruders, snatching several bottles of fine burgundy. Others fought to gain their share. The drunken horde gorged itself in an orgy of alcohol. A worker named No, discovering the revelers sprawled along the floor in puddles of red wine, alertly summoned a detachment of the National Guard. The contingent quietly carried the wall safe containing the Crown Jewels on a stretcher to the National Guard headquarters before the revelers awakened.

At headquarters, General Courtais, the National Guard's commanding officer, forced open the locked strongbox. Due to the explosive political situation, General Courtais ordered those present to stuff the jewels into their pockets without inventorying the contents. "Follow me," he shouted. Carrying Charles X's crown containing the Regent Diamond under his arm, the General hurried through a subterranean passage to the Chief-of-Staff's office across the way. National Guard soldiers trailed behind him. Upon command, the soldiers stacked the precious load in a corner of the office and covered it with a tablecloth. Two burly soldiers guarded the treasure. Later in the day, the men filled five bags with the jewels, loaded the bags onto a furniture van, and, escorted by a detachment of the National Guard, carried the treasure to the safety of the vaults at the Ministry of Finance. On March 12th, an inventory indicated a hat button made of brilliant-cut diamonds and two rose-cut diamond pendants had disappeared. Despite a thorough search, the three items, valued at more than 300,000 francs, remained missing.

Charles X had made a dignified exit from France following his abdication. His successor, Louis Philippe, departed like a common felon. He fled with his Queen through a back door of the Tuileries. He hid in a gardener's cottage until the British

smuggled him and his wife out of the country in disguise under
the pseudonym of Mr. and Mrs. Smith. Louis Philippe spent his
final years living *incognito* in England as the Count of Neuilly.
He died on August 26, 1850, at the age of seventy-seven.

With Louis Philippe out of power a group of radical lawyers
and journalists seized the *Hotel de Ville*, forming a provisional
republican government. Revolutionaries struggled against socialists for control of the new France. Both sides failed. On December 10, 1848, weary of both the socialists and the revolutionaries,
the middle class of France elected Prince Louis Napoleon President of the Republic by an overwhelming majority.

NINE

On April 20, 1808, Hortense Beauharnais, the wife of Louis Napoleon, King of Holland, gave birth to a third son, Louis Napoleon Bonaparte. Six years earlier in 1802, Napoleon I, then Emperor of France, had arranged the marriage of his younger brother Louis and his stepdaughter Hortense to enhance the family's political prestige in Europe. By 1806, Napoleon I had placed his brother on the throne of Holland as a puppet ruler. However, Emperor Napoleon I had difficulty controlling his brother, whose marriage with Hortense proved a disaster.

Louis Napoleon, a physical and emotional wreck, suffered from a paralysis handicapping the fingers on his right hand. Vertigo, headaches and chronic depression racked his brain. Dealing with his ministers irked him, and he detested his wife. In 1810, after a tumultuous marriage, the royal couple separated. Louis refused to provide for or see his son for fourteen years, forcing Hortense to turn to her stepfather, Emperor Napoleon I for the upkeep of her young family. The Emperor provided Hortense with 2,000,000 francs per year. The solitude of an empty bed bored the beautiful Hortense, who became the mistress of Count Charles de Flahaut. In 1811, she gave birth to the Count's bastard son.

Following Emperor Napoleon I's exile to Elba, Hortense and her family moved to Augsburg in Germany. As the years passed, her son Louis Napoleon matured into a highly intelligent, introspective and unattractive adult. His long torso sprouted above squat legs. An enormous nose and thick moustache crowned his oversized head. Later, Prince Louis added the distinctive Vandyke beard he wore throughout the remainder of his life.

Adventuresome in spirit although outwardly quiet, Louis Napoleon and his older brother joined a revolutionary movement to expel the Pope from Rome. When the attempt failed, soldiers captured and imprisoned the two brothers. Louis's brother died in jail from complications caused by measles. Following the young man's death, Hortense rushed to the authorities to beg for the release of her only surviving son, since Louis's second brother had died previously during a childhood illness. Hortense's entreaty succeeded. The Prince's jailers released the young man to his mother.

With the death of Emperor Napoleon I's son on July 22, 1832, Prince Louis Napoleon officially assumed the role of heir to his uncle's throne. He published the pamphlet *Political Reveries*, detailing his program to regenerate France.

In order to draw attention to the Napoleonic cause, Prince Louis initiated a revolt of the Strasbourg garrison in 1836. The mutiny failed. King Louis Philippe, then King of France, ordered Louis Napoleon exiled to Norfolk, Virginia, aboard the ship *Andromede*. In 1837, Prince Louis violated his exile by returning to Switzerland without King Louis Philippe's approval, ostensibly to visit his dying mother. In actuality, Louis returned to pursue his political career. Before sailing for Europe, Louis sent a letter of apology to the American President Martin Van Buren as "one head of state to another" for neglecting to call on him. Of course, Van Buren had never requested any such visit.

When King Louis Philippe learned of Louis's escape to Switzerland, he directed his police to arrest the Prince. Louis fled to England to avoid arrest. In London, Prime Minister Disraeli befriended Louis, helping him publish the 50,000 word *Des Idees Napoleoniennes*, an elaborate defense of Emperor Napoleon I's ideas.

On May 26, 1840, the French government shipped Napoleon I's ashes from Saint Helena on the ship *Belle Poule* to be buried at *Les Invalides* in Paris. At first, Louis plotted to hijack his uncle's

ashes from the ship. Instead, he decided on a frontal attack. He
would return to France and raise an army. Sporting a diamond-
studded eagle snatching a thunderbolt of rubies to symbolize
the Napoleonic dynasty, Louis chartered the paddleship *Edinburgh*
Castle to cross the English channel. Aboard ship Louis addressed
his fifty-six followers:

"Companions of my destiny, it is for France that we are
bound. Our success is certain. Support me bravely, and in a few
days we shall be in Paris; history will relate that it was with a
mere handful of gallant fellows such as you are that I shall have
accomplished this great and glorious enterprise."

When this ragtag assortment reached the fort at Boulogne,
Louis boldly approached the captain of the barracks. "Captain,
I am Prince Louis Napoleon. Join us, and there is nothing
which you may not have."

As Louis prepared to promote the captain to a colonel, the
officer barked: "Prince or no prince—get the hell out of my
barracks! And take your idiot friends with you!"

In the ensuing confusion, both sides fired shots. Louis Napoleon and his band found themselves in the town jail. On August
12, 1845, the local authorities delivered Louis to Paris to stand
trial for treason. At the trial, Louis defended his actions:

"I stand before you as the representative of a principle, a
cause and a defeat. The principle is the sovereignty of the
people; the cause is that of the Empire; the defeat is Waterloo.
You have acknowledged the principle; you have served the
cause; as for the defeat, it is for you to avenge it."

On the very day the government deposited Napoleon I's
ashes at *Les Invalides*, Louis Philippe's court sentenced Louis
Napoleon to life imprisonment in the fortress at the city of
Ham. There, the Prince wrote *Extinction du Pauperisme*, a self-
promotional pamphlet detailing his program for the extinction
of poverty.

With the passage of time, Louis Philippe's government dis-
counted the threat of a Louis Napoleon-inspired uprising. The
"Pretender" became a joke rather than a serious contender.
Gradually, security at Ham eased. After more than five years in

prison, Louis Napoleon escaped with the aid of a few loyal followers who smuggled the necessary props into his room. Disguising himself in a black wig and workman's clothing, the Prince stuck a pipe in his mouth and calmly walked out of the lightly guarded prison carrying a plank of wood. Although Louis Napoleon developed severe rheumatism at Ham, his ambition and drive survived any discomfort.

Following King Louis Philippe's abdication and flight from France in 1848, Prince Louis Napoleon returned to Paris. "I hurry from exile to place myself under the banner of the newly proclaimed Republic," he wrote the provisional government. "I believe that from time to time men are created whom I should describe as providential into whose hands are committed the fates of their countries. I believe myself to be one of these men." The government declined his help.

Refusing to accept this initial rejection, Prince Napoleon appeared before the assembly to argue his position as Napoleon I's legitimate heir and the logical political leader of France. He cut such a sorry figure the opposition neglected to take him seriously. However, the country remembered and relished France's greatness under his uncle. The voters ignored the assembly and elected Louis Napoleon President of the Republic in a stunning upset in the election of December 10th, 1850. On the 20th of the month, Louis swore "to remain faithful to the Democratic Republic, to regard as enemies of the nation all those who may attempt by illegal means to change the form of the established government." Despite this oath, Louis Napoleon secretly vowed to himself to exchange his presidency for a throne.

One year later, after a systematic program culminating in a *coup d'etat* on December 2nd, 1851, Louis Napoleon set up a dictatorship. In the election of 1852, the people granted Louis his wish, voting to crown him Napoleon III, Emperor of France.

During the period prior to the *coup d'etat* known as the Second Republic, the Crown Jewels remained unused in the Treasury. With the onset of the Second Empire, the legislature voted to place the Crown Jewels at the Emperor's disposal.

The Emperor recognized the necessity of finding a wife to

provide him with an heir. On January 29th, 1853, after a suitable
courtship, the forty-five-year-old Napoleon III married the beautiful twenty-seven-year-old Spaniard, Eugenie de Montejo, Countess of Teba. Eugenie's rich copper hair, almond-shaped blue
eyes and glorious complexion contrasted strongly with the
Emperor's dull palor and grey, lusterless eyes. Her natural
gracefulness accentuated his stoutness and lack of height. Under-
standibly, Eugenie's youth and vitality captivated the Emperor.

Shortly after the marriage, Napoleon III appointed the House
of Bapst as Crown Jewelers. The Emperor commissioned the
Bapsts to make his imperial crown and decorations. Since the
Empress requested extensive changes to tailor the remaining
jewels to her taste, the Emperor authorized additional jewelers
including Kramer, Viette, Fester and Lemmonier to create her
crown diadem, comb, fan, belt and pins. Alfred Bapst designed
the balance of Eugenie's jewelry, comprising such pieces as two
large shoulder knots, an ivy-leaf ornament and a broach containing a 337-carat pearl known as the *Regente*.

During the Paris Exhibition of 1855, Napoleon displayed
several pieces from the Crown Jewels, including the Regent
Diamond.

As Napoleon's dreams of Empire expanded and his ardor for
his wife cooled following the birth of their son Louis, Napoleon III
sought gratification elsewhere. "As a rule, the man makes the
attack," the Emperor jokingly explained, "but I defend myself
and sometimes surrender."

Eugenie's moralistic Catholic upbringing bristled at her
husband's infidelities. "How dare you treat me this way?" she
would scream at him. Eugenie consoled herself with elaborate
clothing and jewelry. Charles Worth created magnificent dresses
for her. In 1863, the Empress ordered a Russian tiara of exquisite proportions containing 1,200 brilliant and 442 rose-cut diamonds from the Bapsts.

In 1867, Alfred Bapst designed and Frederic Bapst created
the Meander Tiara. This headpiece contained a socket in which
the Regent Diamond, then valued at $5,000,000, could be placed.
The Tiara derived its name from the Maiandros River in Greece,

whose serpentine curves inspired an ornamental band composed of regular lines set at right angles to each other. The Empress wore the Regent in the tiara at the *Exposition Universelle* of 1867, dazzling the visiting dignitaries with her beauty, jewelry and regal being.

Court records indicate the Empress wore the Regent frequently. In her memoirs, *My Years in Paris,* Pauline Metternich, an Austrian aristocrat and friend to Eugenie, described a party for forty guests at the Emperor's hunting lodge in Compeigne where the Empress wore the Regent with a tuft of feathers in her hair. Eugenie's jewelry and clothing surpassed that of any other monarch in the world for style and elegance.

While Eugenie added to her jewelry collection, her husband annexed Nice and Savoy at Austria's expense. Despite such outward successes, weaknesses in France's armor quickly surfaced. By the end of the 1860's the Emperor's health had eroded. Worn out by sensual excesses and an inflamed bladder, Napoleon struggled to find the stamina to face the turmoil of a troubled reign. A potential war with Prussia added to the Emperor's woes.

In the midst of France's growing difficulties, Eugenie continued to entertain lavishly. Following a May 9, 1870, plebiscite confirming Napoleon's monarchy, the Empress held a great ball at the *Salle des Etats* of the Louvre to celebrate. The Emperor wore a general's uniform and sat quietly. Eugenie appeared in a gold silk gown and a small hat containing the Regent Diamond surrounded by osprey feathers. The Empress looked radiant, the great room sparkling with her glow.

The years had aged Napoleon III. A young Englishman visiting Paris described the weakened Emperor's condition as follows:

> On a bench overlooking the gravel in front of the Tuileries sat a very tired old gentleman, rather hunched together, and looking decidingly ill. I do not think I would have recognized him but for his spiked moustache. Behind him stood the Empress Eugenie, a splendid figure, straight as a dart, and to my eyes the most beautiful thing I had ever seen.

Napoleon III had suffered numerous setbacks in prestige, each one showing on his face and body. After the Mexican government had overthrown and executed his friend and ally Maximillian, the Emperor's popularity ebbed. The Empress, caught up in a fervor of patriotism, called for war against Prussia to avenge the French loss of Mexico. Eugenie believed a victory for Catholic France over Protestant Prussia would re-establish her country's supremacy and rally public support.

On the morning of July 28th, 1870, Napoleon III, assisted by his fourteen-year-old son Louis, reached the train depot in preparation to meet the French army under Marshal MacMahon at Metz against Prussia. Eugenie joined them at the station to bid farewell. Although fall was more than a month away, the weather had soured. A harsh wind chilled the leaves from the trees. As the Empress made the sign of the cross on her son's forehead, she shuddered from the cold. The hint of a tear formed in the corner of her eye. When the train chugged away, the taste of fear impeded her breathing.

At Metz, poor health had made the Emperor indecisive. He had difficulty sitting upright on a horse. Lacking both physical strength and military experience, he became a liability to the army. On August 7th, Marshal MacMahon's army suffered a devastating defeat at Froeschwiller. The French losses exceeded 11,000 men. Defeatism spread through the troops like cancer. By the 9th, word reached Paris the Prussians had decimated MacMahon's army.

On the 10th, the Minister of the Imperial House realized the Crown Jewels would be unsafe at the Tuileries. Therefore, he packed the treasure in a wooden box marked with an anchor at each corner, sealing it with the signs of the Treasury of the Privy Purse, the Crown Jeweler and the Minister of the Imperial household. The Minister ordered the box delivered under armed guard to the Public Treasury at the Ministry of Finance. At the end of August, fearing a German invasion, he asked M. Rolland, the Governor of the Bank of France, to accept responsibility for the Crown Jewels.

Rolland hid the box holding the Crown Jewels including the

Regent Diamond inside one of the bank's outer containers stamped with the words *"Chaines d'Assemblage"* and "Special Projectiles." As an added precaution, the bank shipped the container on a train to Brest along with the bank's bullion. Two bank agents guarded the cargo. At Brest, the agents stored the precious cargo at an armory until the end of the war.

Following his army's initial defeat, logic told Napoleon III to retreat to Paris. Leadership, numbers and equipment favored the enemy. However, word from the Empress urged him to hold his position at Sedan. On August 27th, anticipating the worst, the Emperor sent his son to a safer position behind the lines. Surrounded by Prussian forces on three sides, Marshal Mac-Mahon advised the Emperor to escape while there was still time. Napoleon steadfastly refused. "I have decided not to separate my lot from that of the army."

Rouging his face to hide its sickly pallor, Napoleon donned a general's uniform. Mounting his horse Phoebe, he rode into battle. Bullets whizzed by his head, killing an officer at his side. With every step his horse took, pain echoed throughout the Emperor's body. Courting danger throughout the day, he displayed remarkable valor against overwhelming odds.

By September 2nd, the Prussians had defeated the French at Sedan. The battle closed at 4:15 P.M. with Napoleon ordering the white flag of surrender hoisted. The Emperor and his army of 80,000 surrendered to the Prussians under Bismarck. Napoleon wrote to his wife: "The army has been defeated and is captive. I myself am a prisoner." The Emperor remained a prisoner at Wilhelmshohe Castle near Cassel in Westphalia until war's end.[29]

In Paris, Eugenie bravely faced the crisis. While members of the legislature urged her to abdicate, she sat passively in her black dress and violet shawl listening to the arguments, never revealing "how each sentence uncovered a new danger and each word struck a knife into my anguished heart." The sorrows of defeat already had begun to line her face. Yet, her courage remained. She recognized the dynasty had been lost. On September 4th, with the Prussians nearing the heart of France, Eugenie agreed to abdicate, and the Second Empire fell.

As mobs fought to enter the Tuileries, Eugenie imagined a fate similar to that experienced by Marie Antoinette almost a century earlier. She entrusted her personal jewelry to her friend Pauline Metternich for safekeeping. Wearing a black hat with a veil, she fled through the vast courtyard formed by the wings of the Louvre and the Tuileries. The Empress entered an awaiting carriage with her friend and companion Madame LeBreton. Appearing at the home of her dentist Dr. Evans, she broke down and sobbed. "I am no longer fortunate. The evil days have come, and I am left alone." Assisted by Dr. Evans, Empress Eugenie departed Paris on September 5th carrying only a handkerchief and a small handbag.

With the exception of her initial outbreak, the Empress's coolness amazed Dr. Evans. He recalled seeing her the previous year on a state visit to Constantinople enroute to the inauguration of the Suez Canal "in an evening dress, a light mantilla over her head, wearing a diadem containing the Regent Diamond." Now in the midst of a downpour of rain, she sat huddled in a corner, drenched to the skin, awaiting a change of carriages.

Empress Eugenie left France for England on September 7th in a yacht, crossing the channel during a violent storm. "The little vessel was jumping on the waves like a cork. I thought we were lost," she later wrote. In fact, that very night another ship crossing the channel, the *HMS Captain,* sank with the loss of 500 men. At dawn, Eugenie landed safely near Ryde at the Isle of Wright.

After reuniting with her son Louis at a hotel near Hasting, Eugenie wrote Tsar Alexander II of Russia and Emperor Franz Josef of Austria requesting help in securing an honorable peace for France.

During the Empress's escape, a full-scale insurrection erupted in Paris. A mob burst into the Treasury searching for the Crown Jewels. All they found were models set with fake stones, leading to a rumor the Empress had stolen the Crown Jewels for herself. When the provisional government learned the jewelry had been moved, delegates hastened to the Bank of France, demanding the Crown Jewels. The bankers refused to divulge their whereabouts, and the treasure remained safely in Brest for several months.

On January 28, 1871, France and Germany signed an armistice. The National Assembly ceded Alsace and part of Lorraine, including the fortesses of Metz and Strasbourg, to Prussia. In addition, France agreed to pay a substantial indemnity. On March 20th, with the war ended, the Bank of France returned the bullion from Brest to Paris. For political reasons the Republic placed the Crown Jewels in the hold of a ship named the *Borda* until 1872. As additional security, an admiral kept the frigate *Hermione* in constant readiness to sail for Saigon with the Crown Jewels in case of revolution or another German attack. When the Crown Jewels returned to Paris in 1872, a commission carefully checked to be certain all were there before depositing them in the Ministry of Finance for safekeeping.

After the formal signing of the treaty in mid-March, the Prussians released Napoleon III. The deposed Emperor traveled to Dover, where his wife and son greeted him. Upon receiving her personal jewelry from her friend Pauline Metternich, the Empress sold several items to help support her husband and son.

The family retired to Chiselhurst in Kent. Emperor Napoleon spent his leisure composing two pamphlets entitled *Military Forces of France 1870* and *The Campaign of 1870*, explaining the last year of his reign. "A sovereign can offer no excuses, he can plead no extenuating circumstances. It is his highest prerogative to shoulder all the responsibilities incurred by those who have served him or those who have betrayed him," he wrote. The Emperor never complained about his downfall. He dreamed of a return to power, but recognized he was too ill. Eugenie had a difficult time matching her husband's resignation and forgiveness. She planned for the day on which her son would rule France.

Napoleon III had an honest love of humanity so long as it did not interfere with his ambition. He built a public health system, roads, sewers, railroads, churches, hospitals and theaters.

He tore down disease-ridden slums, changing the fabric of life in Paris. Commerce and trading flourished during his reign.

On January 2, 1873, doctors removed kidney stones from the Emperor. The rigors of the surgery attacked his weakened body. Napoleon III died on January 9th of complications from the operation. The Emperor's son, Prince Louis, died in 1879 at the age of twenty-three during hand-to-hand combat against knife-wielding African Zulus, effectively ending the Napoleonic dynasty. Louis was buried beside his father in a small Catholic church in Chislehurst.

Empress Eugenie survived her husband by almost fifty years until her ninety-fourth year, although she often said, "I died in 1870 after my husband's defeat at Sedan." Shortly before her death in 1920, she thanked God for allowing her to live long enough to see France defeat Germany in World War I. "It almost makes up for everything," she sighed, but how she wished her son and husband could have shared the victory.

TEN

THE ARMISTICE OF 1871 ended Franco-German hostilities, bringing peace to most of Europe. With the threat of war ended, the French provisional government transferred the Crown Jewels from Brest to the cellar in the Ministry of Justice in Paris for safekeeping.

On June 7, 1878, a deputy of the Third Republic named Benjamin Raspail proposed the sale of the Crown Jewels to raise funds to cover the costs of the lost war. Raspail viewed the Crown Jewels as a functionless reminder of the previous monarchy. Napoleon III had brought France shame and defeat. Raspail believed the government should profit from the sale of the jewels worn by Napoleon III and his wife. Coincidentally, thirty years earlier, Raspail's father had suggested the Crown Jewels be sold following King Louis Philippe's downfall in 1848 for identical reasons.

The younger Raspail's motion languished in the Assembly for almost four years through a series of long and tedious discussions until approved on June 20, 1882, by a vote of 342 to 85. The Senate ratified the Assembly's bill on December 7, 1886, after almost four more years of debate between Royalists and Republicans.

Under the revised version of the bill, the Senate voted to preserve the Regent in the Louvre. The diamond would be public property for all to see and admire, a symbol of the grandeur of France's past. The legislators further specified that the *Cote-de-Bretagne* ruby, the coronation sword of Charles X, and the Reliquary Brooch should join the Regent at the Louvre due to their artistic merit. Furthermore, the Senate assigned a few pieces of jewelry with historical or scientific worth to the Natural History Museum and the School of Mines.[30]

The Senate voted to crush the Imperial Crown and the sword of Louis XVIII as bitter reminders of tyranny after removing their precious stones. The scrap gold derived would be sold. The balance of the Crown Jewels were to be auctioned, the proceeds benefiting the government.

Raspail, who held a personal grudge against Napoleon III, demanded the privilege of destroying the Crown. "I myself will break up this Crown and send it to the foundry," he boasted. Unfortunately, Raspail accidentally fell and broke his leg. He had to content himself with receiving the hammer used by his replacement.

Guards shifted the Crown Jewels programed for auction to the *Salle des Etats,* the State Room, in the *Pavillon de Flora,* the Pavillion of Flowers. The treasure remained on display for potential bidders to examine from April 20th through May 12th, 1883. The sale itself lasted from May 12th through the 23rd, attracting buyers from all over the world. The auction netted 6,927,509 francs after all expenses.[31]

Officials relocated the Regent Diamond, the twenty-carat, five-sided pink Hortense Diamond, the coronation sword of Charles X, Louis XV's crown with paste facsimiles of the original stones and several smaller historical pieces from the cellar of the Ministry of Justice to the Louvre's *Galerie d'Apollon,* the Gallery of Apollo.

The idea of using the Louvre for a museum of art and jewelry had originated as early as 1749 during Louis XV's reign. In 1774, King Louis XVI's Director General of Palace and Gardens, the Count of Angiviller, proposed a public showing of the master-pieces from the royal collection, but hordes of giant bats first had to be dislodged before the project could continue. In 1791, the politician Barrere addressed the Revolutionary Assembly: "We must restore the Louvre and turn it into a famous museum." At the instigation of the renowned painter Louis David, the Assembly adopted Barrere's plan on August 10, 1792. One year later, the National Convention decreed, "All works of art seized by the Revolution from convents, churches and former royal palaces should be brought to the Louvre." Thus, in August of 1793, the government exhibited 537 pictures in the building's Grand Gallery.

In 1798, the Louvre displayed antique and Renaissance masterpieces confiscated by Napoleon Bonaparte during his victorious Italian campaign. Horses from Venice and sculptures of Laocoön and the Dying Gaul graced the *Galerie d'Apollon* and the *Salon Carre*. Unfortunately, this plundered art had to be returned to Italy following Bonaparte's downfall in 1814.

Many consider Napoleon Bonaparte to be the founder of the modern day Louvre Museum. During his term as First Consul, the Museum opened three days a week for public viewing. In 1801, the *Cour Carree* held France's first industrial exhibition.

Later, Bonaparte ordered the interior redecoration of the Grand Gallery and the *Cour Carree*. In fact, Napoleon became so attracted to the Louvre that he married his second wife, Marie-Louise, in the *Salon Carre*. One guest wrote: "The magnificent pictures, the fresh decorations, the brilliant jewels, the beautiful women, and, above all, the magical effect of the sunlight penetrating the apertures in the ceiling and the windows in the side walls, produced an effect that is beyond expression."

Following Napoleon's fall, Fontaine carried on the Louvre's expansion. Anti-monarchists invaded the Louvre in 1830, but passed through causing minimal damage. Revolutionaries camped out in the Grand Gallery in 1848. They cooked on the ground floor and transformed the back rooms into a gunpowder magazine and armory. Luckily, the Louvre suffered little permanent damage. On March 24th of 1848, shortly after King Louis Philippe's abdication, the Revolutionary Government temporarily renamed the Louvre the People's Palace. During a brief period in June the Louvre became a casualty station.

A government decree dated March 12, 1852, ordered the completion of the Louvre. Visconti drew the initial plan, and the first brick was laid on July 25th. When Visconti died in 1854, Lefuel carried on the project. Napoleon III formally inaugurated a redesigned Louvre Museum on August 14, 1857. Embodying four centuries of French architecture, the Louvre remains one of the most beautiful buildings in the world and the *Galerie d'Apollon* a fitting home for the Regent.

Charles LeBrun created the *Galerie d'Apollon*'s decor in the sixteenth century during the reign of the Sun King, Louis XIV. LeBrun's murals and sculptures portray the times of the day, the months of the year and the signs of the zodiac in rococo splendor. Twelve windows light the 201-by-31-feet room balanced by thirteen doors on the opposite side.

LeBrun himself painted *Le Reveil des Eaux*, Water's Awakening, *L'Aurore*, Daybreak, accidentally destroyed in the eighteenth century, *Le Soir*, Evening, and *La Nuit*, Night. The artist Jacques Gervaise, who died in 1670, painted eight of the twelve months of the year, the two first and the six last. Jean-Baptiste Monnoyer painted the flowers framing the months. Francois Girardon, Thomas Regnauldin and the Marcy brothers created the sculptures interspersed throughout the room. Unfortunately, Versailles monopolized Lebrun's time before he could complete the Gallery.

During Louis XV and Louis XVI's reign, artists painted *L'Automne*, *l'Ete*, *L'Hiver* and *Le Printemps* — Autumn, Summer, Winter and Spring. In 1819, the Louvre added a handsome grill with a snake motif taken from the Lafitte Mansion to the entryway of the Gallery.

The National Assembly voted on December 7, 1848, to complete the *Galerie d'Apollon*'s restoration. Felix Durban headed the project. Years of abuse had seriously damaged the Gallery's walls. Paintings and sculptures were taken down and cleaned. George Poppleton restored several mythological works. Missing paintings were completed. Joseph Guichard executed the mural *Le Reveil de la Terre*, Earth's Awakening, based on LeBrun's original design. Charles-Louis Muller painted a new *L'Aurore*, Daybreak, from an engraving by Saint-Andre. Finally, by an order of March 8, 1850, Eugene Delacroix painted the giant 26-by-24-feet *Apollon Vainqueur du Serpent Python*, Apollo Defeating the

Serpent, in the center of the ceiling. On June 5th, 1851, Prince Louis Napoleon inaugurated the newly redecorated *Galerie d'Apollon.*

After Delacroix completed his monumental painting in August, the Gallery reopened to the public in October of 1851. Work began immediately on a series of twenty-eight paintings representing the sovereigns and artists who had worked on the Louvre. These portraits separate the various doorways and windows, adding further balance to the room. The pictures include Louis XIV, LeBrun and Eugene Appert. Ironically, in 1890, for political reasons, the authorities removed a painting of Napoleon III, the Emperor responsible for the renovation of the *Gallerie d'Apollon,* replacing it with Henri IV, the ruler of France between 1689 and 1710.

In 1861, three vitrines were placed in the center of the gallery. Five side vitrines and two marble inlaid tables also were added.

The Regent remained in the *Galerie d'Apollon* until 1940. The onset of World War II and the German advance forced the French government to remove all the treasures from the Louvre to a safer spot. Officials expeditiously packed 6,000 crates of artwork, antiques and valuables for consignment to eighty depositories throughout the country. Under absolute secrecy museum officials hid the Regent in an old box and placed it in the base of a fireplace at the *Chateau de Chambord* during the Nazi occupation. In September of 1945, following the German defeat and the liberation of Paris, the Regent returned to the Louvre.

Once the diamond had been returned to the *Galerie d'Apollon,* the Louvre's directors became concerned with the Regent's safety. Louis Devaux, the president of Cartier in Paris, related: "Had anything happened to it, there would be nothing that looked like it or would represent it. We didn't even have a good picture of it to show the cut."

Therefore, Devaux received a commission to cut three replicas of the Regent from crystal. Devaux described the thrill of holding the famous diamond in his hand. "Actually," he confessed, "the models really looked better than the original since the real stone reflected the gold from the ceilings and walls of this very ornate gallery, giving the white stone yellow reflections, which, of course, did not occur with the crystal."

In January of 1962, the Louvre exposition featured "Ten Centuries of French Jewelry." For the first time since the theft of the jewels from the *Garde Meuble* in 1793, the Regent, the Sancy and the Great Blue, now known as the Hope Diamond, were reunited in one location.

Today, the Regent remains in the *Galerie d'Apollon*, centered in Vitrine VII, a glass case about the size of an orange crate. The glass top rests on an elaborate pedestal in the center of the room, allowing viewers to walk around it. A low metal railing has been added for additional security. This railing hides a square opening in the floor. At night the case goes through the floor to a secured vault in the basement.

A sign on the vitrine lists the Regent as 136⅞ carats. However, these are ancient carats. The actual weight is 140.64 carats. Daniel Alcouffe, the Curator in Chief of Objects of Art of the Louvre, lists the dimensions of the Regent as 31.58 millimeters high by 28.87 wide by 20.6 deep, exceptionally large for an almost flawless diamond.

Vitrine VII also includes the 55-carat, pear-shaped Sancy Diamond to the Regent's lower right, the 20¾-carat pink Hortensia to its lower left, and the 105-carat, dragon-shaped *Cote-de-Bretagne* ruby directly beneath the Regent. Pictures of the architect Jules Mansart and the sculptor Jean Goujon hang on either side of the wall behind the case.

Vitrine IX contains the Crown of Louis XV, cast by Augustin Duflos in 1722, based on the design of Claude Ronde. The vermeil headpiece contains paste replicas of the Regent and the Sancy, the original stones having been removed in 1729.

Upon visiting the Louvre, one can easily miss the Regent among the larger and more imposing art works such as the Mona Lisa, Winged Victory or Venus from Melos. The magnificent *Galerie d'Apollon*, with its marble inlaid tables, crystal and gold vases, golden sceptres, massive murals and elegant sculptures and paintings, dwarfs the Regent. Compared to its sister diamonds, the Koh-i-noor in the Queen Mother's Crown at the

Tower of London and the Hope in an elaborate necklace at the Smithsonian, the Regent sits almost naked in the weakly lighted Vitrine VII.

However, the Regent Diamond's history, perfection of cut, size, crystal color and clarity make it one of the Louvre's richest prizes, a monument to the past greatness of France's kings and queens.

From the bandage of a Sudra's leg to the quiet showcase in the Louvre, the Regent Diamond has traveled a long and adventuresome journey. It has earned its resting place among the treasures of France.

Genealogy of the French Royal Family

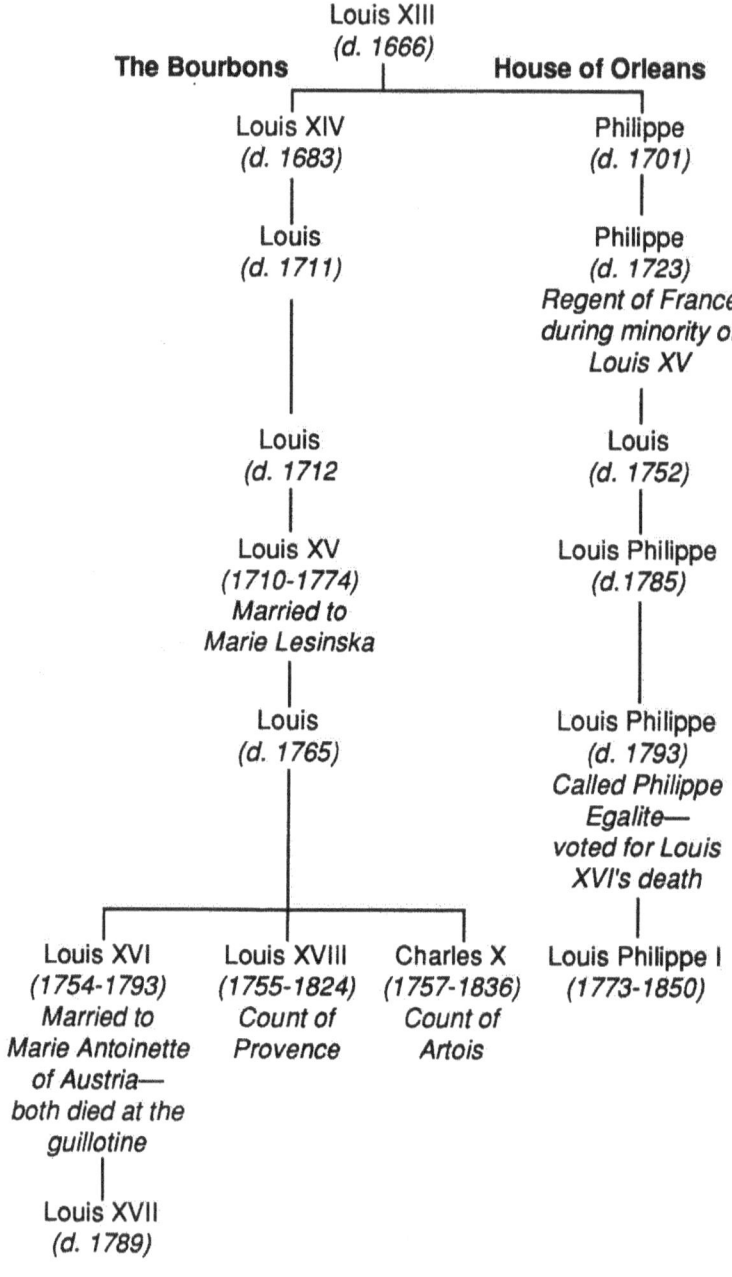

Louis XIII
(d. 1666)

The Bourbons   **House of Orleans**

The Bourbons	House of Orleans
Louis XIV *(d. 1683)*	Philippe *(d. 1701)*
Louis *(d. 1711)*	Philippe *(d. 1723)* *Regent of France during minority of Louis XV*
Louis *(d. 1712*	Louis *(d. 1752)*
Louis XV *(1710-1774)* *Married to Marie Lesinska*	Louis Philippe *(d.1785)*
Louis *(d. 1765)*	Louis Philippe *(d. 1793)* *Called Philippe Egalite— voted for Louis XVI's death*

Louis XVI
(1754-1793)
*Married to
Marie Antoinette
of Austria—
both died at the
guillotine*

Louis XVIII
(1755-1824)
*Count of
Provence*

Charles X
(1757-1836)
*Count of
Artois*

Louis Philippe I
(1773-1850)

Louis XVII
(d. 1789)

1701   A Sudra worker discovers the 426-carat diamond in the Parteal Mine. Thomas Pitt, the Governor of Fort Saint George, purchases the stone.

1702   Thomas Pitt's son takes the rough diamond to England for recutting.

1715   Phillipe, the Regent of France, purchases the Pitt Diamond, now weighing slightly over 140 carats. The stone is renamed the Regent Diamond.

1722   King Louis XV wears the Regent at his coronation.

1774   Louis XV dies. His grandson Louis XVI is crowned king. Louis XVI's wife Marie Antoinette wears the Regent.

1792   The Regent Diamond is stolen from the *Garde Meuble.*

1793   The Regent is recovered. Louis XVI is beheaded.

1799   Napoleon Bonaparte is named First Consul of France. He wears the Regent in the hilt of his sword.

1814   Emperor Napoleon I (Napoleon Bonaparte) exiled to Elba. His wife Marie-Louise turns over the sword to the provisional government. Louis XVIII becomes king.

1815   Napoleon escapes from Elba and returns to France on March 1st. Louis XVIII flees the country. Following his defeat at Waterloo, Napoleon is permanently exiled to St. Helena. Louis XVIII returns.

1824   Louis XVIII dies. Charles X succeeds his brother.

1825   Charles X wears the Regent in his coronation crown.

1830   Charles X abdicates. Louis Philippe I becomes King of France.

1848   Louis Philippe I abdicates. Louis Napoleon is named President of France.

1852   Louis Napoleon becomes Napoleon III.

1867   Alfred Bapst designs the Meander Tiara to hold the Regent for Napoleon III's wife.

1870   Napoleon III abdicates following his surrender to the Prussians. The Regent is held at Brest for security.

1872   The Regent returns to Paris. Eventually, the stone is stored at the Louvre.

1940   At the onset of World War II, the Regent is moved to the Chateau Chambord to protect it against the Nazi occupation.

1945   The Regent returns to the Louvre.

1. Queen Elizabeth I granted the original monopoly charter for the East India Company on December 31, 1600. The English contended with the Dutch, French and Portuguese merchant adventurers for supremacy in India. In addition, the Company struggled with English interlopers who operated outside the charter. Competing Hindu and Moslem provincial governors created another source of conflict. Despite these difficulties, the Company's exports of silk, cotton and gems increased dramatically during the first half of the eighteenth century.
2. In India, a Sudra belongs to the laboring caste. The three other major castes include the Brahmans (priests and scholars), the Kshatriyas (warriors and rules) and the Vaisyas (farmers and business people).
3. According to Jacques Lagrand, the Sudra discovered the diamond in 1698 although most historians accept 1701.
4. Baber became the first Mogul emperor in India, initiating his reign in 1526. His son Humayum and grandson Akbar succeeded him. Jahangir, Jahan and Aurangzeb continued the bloodline. Following Aurangzeb's death in 1707 at the age of eighty-nine, the Mogul Empire declined rapidly. By the middle of the eighteenth century, the Moguls became mere figureheads under English control.

5. Actually, diamonds form under great heat and pressure deep within the earth's surface.

6. Jamchund is sometimes referred to as Ramchund.

7. Regarding Jane, Sir Tresham Lever in *The House of Pitt* states: "The exact relationship to Vincent and Edwards is not clear. Possibly she was a niece of their wives. Her grandmother was Margaret Stuart, Countess of Moray, whose father was an illegitimate son of James V of Scotland and therefore half-brother to Mary, Queen of Scots."

8. A Mangelin is an Indian unit of measurement that varies in standard from one to one and three-quarters of a carat. The author has modernized Pitt's spelling to make his letters more readable.

9. Evans refers to the War of the Spanish Succession, in which Louis XIV of France stood against England and most of Europe.

10. The gem historian Edwin Streeter stated that the British Museum housed one of the crystal models of the Pitt diamond. The writer Murray indicated the British Museum also contained a second model cast in lead.

11. Edwin Streeter, author of *The Great Diamonds of the World*, lists the purchase price as 135,000 pounds instead of 125,000. Streeter's figure includes 5,000 pounds for negotiations, a euphemism for the bribe paid to Law for his part in encouraging the Regent to make the purchase.

12. Louis de Rouvry, the Duke of Saint-Simon, died in Paris on March 2nd, 1755, during his eightieth year, outliving most of his generation and the prosperity of his house.

13. Like the Regent, the fifty-five carat pear-shaped Sancy Diamond had a colorful history. Nicholas Harlai, Seigneur de Sancy and ambassador to the Ottoman Empire, purchased the stone in 1570 in Constantinople. Sancy lent the diamond to King Henry III of France for the hat he always wore to cover his bald head. In 1604, Sancy sold the diamond to King James I of England. In 1688, the deposed King James II of England sold the Sancy to Louis XIV of France for 25,000 pounds.

14. The works of the famous jeweler Georges-Frederic Stras, who was born in Strassbourg in 1700, excel in the art of painted stones.

15. The inventory of 1791 valued the unmounted stones at 23,922,197 francs, or approximately $5,250,000, and the mounted jewelry and other art objects at 5,186,236 francs, or approximately $1,100,000.

16. The Society of the Jacobins, known as the Friends of Liberty and Equality, evolved from a discussion group into a radical association of anti-monarchists. The Jacobins spawned the Reign of Terror under Jean-Paul Marat and his successor, Maximilien Robespierre. Following Robespierre's fall, the Jacobin Club closed.

17. Edwin Streeter, the author of *The Great Diamonds of the World*, related a somewhat implausible story concerning the curator of the *Garde-Meuble*'s arrest. The curator Sargeant announced he had a special magnet to locate the stolen gems. The gullible authorities escorted Sargeant to the *Alee des Veuves* and blindfolded him. Without hesitation, Sargeant pointed to the foot of a tree, where diggers uncovered several stolen diamonds.

18. Edwin Streeter wrote a different explanation: "Some of the objects were in a ditch on the *Allee des Veuves, Champs-Elysees*. Here were found amongst other things the famous Regent Diamond and the Abbe Suger's Chalice." Streeter stated a criminal named Baba, accused of forgery in 1804, admitted to burying the Regent after receiving "the promise of a free pardon, a promise which was faithfully kept."

19. Eric Bruton in *Legendary Gems* asserted the *Cote-de-Bretagne* was a red spinel rather than a ruby. Jacques Buay carved the dragon's head and body to conceal unsightly holes.

20. The 68-carat Great Blue was recut into the 44.5-carat Hope Diamond, now found in the Smithsonian Museum in Washington, D.C., as well as several smaller diamonds.

21. The French government failed to redeem the Sancy, which passed into the possession of the widow of King Charles IV of Spain. The diamond later was sold to the Russian royal

family. In 1867, the jewelry firm of Bapst offered the diamond for sale at the Paris Exhibition for a price of 1,000,000
francs. The Maharajah of Patiala purchased it to wear in his
turban. In 1889, William Waldorf Astor bought the diamond for his wife. In 1978, the Astor family sold the Sancy
to the Bank of France for $1,000,000.00. Today the Sancy
may be viewed in the *Galerie d'Apollon* at the Louvre
Museum.

22. Bapst in *History of the Crown Jewels of France* stated M. Faye,
President of the Bureau of Geography, whose father knew
Vanlenberghem, had related this story to him.

23. Frances Winwar in *Napoleon and the Battle of Waterloo* stated
Napoleon wore the Regent in his plumed hat at the coronation. Since the Regent was set in his consular sword at that
time, this version appears improbable.

24. In 1962, Mrs. Herbert May presented Marie-Louise's necklace to the Smithsonian Institution in Washington, D.C.

25. Conflicting stories have circulated concerning the way the
Regent returned to Paris following the Empress's flight.
Some believe Marie-Louise took the diamond to Austria, and
her father, Emperor Francis II, later forced her to give back
the stone to France. Others believe Dudon confiscated Napoleon's hilt and returned it to the provisional government.

26. An N.W. Ayer press release referring to the Regent dated
June 11, 1962, stated: "Louis XVIII wore it in his cap."
Because Bapst mounted the Regent in a crown, this version
must be incorrect.

27. In 1854, the authorities dismantled Charles X's crown,
relegating the empty frame to the cellar of the Ministry of
Finance. The Crown Jeweler Bapst offered to purchase the
crown, set it with facsimile stones and present it to the
Louvre as a gift. The French leadership objected for political
reasons since the Bourbons were out of favor at that time.

28. The historian Edwin Streeter believed the Regent and the
Crown Jewels remained in the *Garde-Meuble* during Louis
Philippe's reign rather than at the Louvre.

29. Napoleon III's Uncle Jerome, the youngest brother of Napo-

leon I, had ruled Wesphalia several decades earlier. A portrait of Emperor Napoleon III's mother, Queen Hortense,
hung on the walls of the castle.

30. The Sword of Charles X was stolen from the Louvre during
the night of December 15, 1976.

31. Gross proceeds from the sale were 6,864,050 francs. By
adding the receipts from the gold melted down and a 5
percent commission paid by the buyers, the total reached
7,221,360 francs. After subtracting expenses of 293,851 francs,
the net proceeds became 6,927,509 francs. The government
invested the entire balance in 3 percent bonds. Assuming a
franc equaled approximately $2.50 today, the sale generated
the phenomenal sum of $17,318,772.50.

ABBOTT, JOHN S. C. *Marie Antoinette.* The Circle Publishing Company. New York, New York, 1902.

Alcouffe, Daniel. *Musee du Louvre: La Galerie d'Apollon.* Department des Objets d'Arte. Paris, France, 1985.

Allan, J. *The Cambridge Shorter History of India.* The Macmillan Company. New York, New York, 1934.

Argenzio, Victor. *Diamonds Eternal.* David McKay Company, Inc. New York, New York, 1974.

Aronson, Theo. *The Fall of the Third Napoleon.* Bobbs-Merrill Company, Inc. New York, New York, 1970.

Ayer, N.W. *Notable Diamonds of the World.* New York, New York, 1971.

Balfour, Ian. *Famous Diamonds.* William Collins Sons and Company. London, England, 1987.

Bapst, G. *Histoire des Joyaux de la Couronne de France.* Paris, France, 1889. (Translated with the assistance of Dr. Jesse Mann of Westminster College and Dr. Nanette Solomon.)

Beach, Vincent W. *Charles X of France.* Pruett Publishing Company. Boulder, Colorado, 1971.

Benton, William (Publisher). *Encyclopaedia Britannica.* Encyclopaedia Britannica, Inc. Chicago, Illinois, 1956.

Bernier, Olivier. *Louis the Beloved.* Doubleday and Company. Garden City, New York, 1984.

Brodsky, Alyn. *Imperial Charade.* Bobbs-Merrill Company, Inc. New York, New York, 1978.

Bruton, Eric. *Diamonds.* Chilton Book Company. Radnor, Pennsylvania, 1978.

Bruton, Eric. *Legendary Gems or Gems That Made History.* Chilton Book Company. Radnor, Pennsylvania, 1986.

Carlyle, Thomas. *The French Revolution. Volume 10.* Peter Fenelon Collier. New York, New York, 1897.

Corley, T.A.B. *Democratic Despot. A Life of Napoleon III.* Greenwood Press. Westport, Connecticut, 1974.

Dalton, Sir Cornelius Neale. *The Life of Pitt.* Cambridge University Press. London, England, 1915.

Davis, William Stearns. *A History of France.* The Chautauqua Press. Chautauqua, New York, 1920.

DeGramont, Sanche. *Epitaph For Kings.* G. P. Putnam's Sons. New York, New York, 1967.

Dickens, A.G. *The Courts of Europe — Politics, Patronage and Royalty 1400-1800.* McGraw-Hill. New York, New York, 1977.

Dieulafait, Louis. *Diamonds and Precious Stones.* Scribner, Armstrong and Company. New York, New York, 1874.

Durant, Will and Ariel. *The Story of Civilization. The Age Of Louis XIV.* Simon and Schuster. New York, New York, 1963.

Durant, Will and Ariel. *The Story of Civilization. The Age Of Voltaire.* Simon and Schuster. New York, New York, 1965.

Durant, Will and Ariel. *The Story of Civilization. Rousseau and the Revolution.* Simon and Schuster. New York, New York, 1967.

Ergang, Robert. *Europe from the Renaissance to Waterloo.* D. C. Heath and Company. Boston, Massachusetts, 1954.

Gauthier, Maximilien. *The Louvre Paintings.* Meredith Press. New York, New York, 1962.

Gaxotte, Pierre. *Louis the Fifteenth and His Times.* J.B. Lippincott and Company. Philadelphia, Pennsylvania, 1934.

Godechot, Jacques. *France and the Atlantic Revolution of the Eighteenth Century, 1770-1799.* The Free Press. New York, New York, 1965.

Gooch, G. P. *Louis XV.* Longmans, Green and Company. London, England, 1956.

Guizot, Francois Pierre Guillaume. *A Popular History of France from the Earliest Times. Volume VI.* University Press. Boston, Massachusetts, 1869.

Hedges, William. *The Diary of William Hedges, Esq. During His Agency in Bengal; As Well As on His Voyage Out and Return Overland (1681–1687).* Volumes I, II, and III. Burt Franklin. New York, New York, 1888.

Heiniger, Ernst A. and Jean. *The Great Book of Jewels.* Edita Lausanne. Zurich, Switzerland, 1974.

Herold, Christopher J. *The Horizon Book of the Age of Napoleon.* Harmony Books. New York, New York, 1962.

Jones, William. *Crowns and Coronations.* Chatto and Windus. London, England, 1902.

Laclotte, Michael and Cuzin, Jean-Pierre. *The Louvre.* Scala Books. London, England, 1982.

Legrand, Jacques. *Diamonds: Myth, Magic, and Reality.* Crown Publishers. New York, New York, 1980.

Lever, Sir Tresham. *The House of Pitt.* John Murray. London, England, 1948.

Loomis, Stanley. *Paris in the Terror.* Richardson and Steirman. New York, New York, 1986.

Maurois, Andre. *A History of France.* Translated from French by Henry L. Binsse. Grove Press, Inc. New York, New York, 1960.

Mawe, John. *A Treatise on Diamonds and Precious Stones of the Hindus.* The Ronald Press. New York, New York, 1953.

Perelman, Dale. *Mountain of Light.* Apollo Books. Winona, Minnesota, 1984.

Perkins, James Breck. *France Under the Regency.* Houghton, Mifflin and Company. Cambridge, England, 1892.

Prince Michael of Greece. *Crown Jewels of Europe.* Harper and Row. New York, New York, 1983.

Romier, Lucien. *A History of France.* Saint Martins Press. New York, New York, 1953.

Saint-Simon, Duc. *Memoires Du Duc De Saint-Simon.* Book XIV. Library Hachette Et Cie. Paris, France, 1887.

Severy, Merle. *Great Religions of the World.* National Geographic Society. Washington, D.C., 1978.

Smith, Vincent A. *The Oxford History of India.* University Press. Oxford, England, 1958.

Streeter, Edwin. *The Great Diamonds of the World.* Gryphon Books. Ann Arbor, Michigan, 1971.

Tavernier, Jean Baptiste. *Les Voyages de Jean Baptiste Tavernier 1679 — Travels in India.* Two Volumes. Translated from French by V. Ball. Al-Biruni. Lahore, Pakistan, 1976.

Thiers, Adolp. *The Mississippi Bauble: A Memoir of John Law.* Greenwood Press. New York, New York, 1969.

Twining, Lord. *A History of the Crown Jewels of Europe.* B.T. Batsford Ltd. London, England, 1960.

Walzer, Michael. *Regicide and Revolution — Speeches at the Trial of Louis XVI.* Cambridge University Press. London, England, 1974.

Webster, Nesta H. *Louis XVI and Marie Antoinette Before the Revolution.* G.P. Putnam. New York, New York, 1937.

Weider, Ben and Hapgood, David. *The Murder of Napoleon.* Congdon and Lattes. New York, New York, 1982.

Winwar, Frances. *Napoleon and the Battle of Waterloo.* Random House. New York, New York, 1953.

Wolpert, Stanley. *New History of India.* Oxford University Press. New York, New York, 1977.

Zweig, Stefan. *Marie Antoinette: the Portrait of an Average Woman.* The Viking Press. New York, New York, 1933.

PERIODICALS

Connoisseur. New York, New York, December, 1985.

FMR. New York, New York, December, 1985.

The Diamond News and S.A. Jeweller. Johannesburg, South Africa, June, 1973.

www.ingramcontent.com/pod-product-compliance
Lightning Source LLC
Chambersburg PA
CBHW051418280526
45785CB00003B/1072